Must Try Harder

Adventures in Anxiety

BY PAULA McGUIRE

We are proud to introduce Theinspirationalseries™. Part of the Trigger Press family of innovative mental health books, Theinspirationalseries™ tells the stories of the people who have battled and beaten mental health issues. For more information visit: www.trigger-press.com

THE AUTHOR

Paula McGuire is an adventurer, speaker and author, but, most of all, she's a trier.

For 30 years Paula lived under a rock, somewhere on the outskirts of every social situation, suffering crippling anxiety, panic attacks and depression that would eventually rob her of even the most basic freedoms. After decades of medication and intervention, adventure became Paula's personal therapy in 2012, when she became Paula Must Try Harder, trying the 17 Commonwealth sports, exposing her to constant fear and enabling her to fight her way back into the world.

Ever since, Paula has terrified herself daily in the name of recovery, and now spends all that nervous energy challenging herself to wild exploits and encouraging others to allow a little fear into their days. From skinny-dipping and flying a plane to going shopping on her own, Paula's adventures have covered the bizarre and the banal, and demonstrate that living a happy, full life with anxiety really is possible.

First published in Great Britain 2018 by Trigger Press

Trigger Press is a trading style of Shaw Callaghan Ltd & Shaw Callaghan 23 USA, INC.

The Foundation Centre

Navigation House, 48 Millgate, Newark

Nottinghamshire NG24 4TS UK

www.trigger-press.com

British Library Cataloguing in Publication Data

A CIP catalogue record for this book is available upon request from the British Library

ISBN: 978-1-911246-85-5

This book is also available in the following e-Book formats:

MOBI: 978-1-911246-88-6

EPUB: 978-1-911246-86-2

PDF: 978-1-911246-87-9

Cover design and typeset by Fusion Graphic Design Ltd

Project Management by Out of House Publishing

Printed and bound in Great Britain by Bell & Bain, Glasgow

Paper from responsible sources

www.trigger-press.com

Thank you for purchasing this book. You are making an incredible difference.

Proceeds from all Trigger Press books go directly to The Shaw Mind Foundation, a global charity that focuses entirely on mental health. To find out more about The Shaw Mind Foundation visit, **www.shawmindfoundation.org**

MISSION STATEMENT

Our goal is to make help and support available for every single person in society, from all walks of life. We will never stop offering hope. These are our promises.

Trigger Press and The Shaw Mind Foundation

For Gerry, my courage when I have none.

For Mum, Dad and Donna, who always knew the person I could be.

PROLOGUE

'Let's get started.'

Three innocuous little words slip from a casual tongue. I've heard them before, heralding exams or meetings. But this time, oh God, this time ...

I hesitate.

The artists grip pencils in nimble fingers, wood creaking against graphite in anticipation. They have no idea what shape or form lies beneath this crumpled waffle dressing gown, from the local supermarket's basic range. Hell, I'm not shape. I'm not form. I'm barely even structurally sound at this point. What am I doing here, in the middle of a strange village hall, hemmed in by a circle of baying Botticellis, shivering in spite of the electric heaters pointed in all my varying directions?

These people expect a model, something to sketch that isn't wobbling to the beat of its own shame. My only existing modelling quality is a clay-like consistency. I'm pretty sure they could fashion a decent sculpture from one thigh, but catwalk-ready, I am not. I have scars and knobbles, a complexion so pasty it could fix wallpaper. Shapes like mine need corralling with care and cardigan, not setting free to cavort as they so please.

Perhaps there's still a way out. Maybe I can just dissolve in the pit of bile masquerading as my digestive system, or paddle seaward on the constant stream from my overworked sweat glands.

Someone, please, spare us all this shared experience. Sometimes spirit just isn't worth the Dunkirk.

Sixteen foreheads bob expectantly above mottled easels. I have to do something. Anything. Move, Paula. Fight. Try. Every moment's pause, I'm keeping the life drawing class from their subject.

Dynamic poses, isn't that what the tutor said? So pose, woman – and put some dynamism into it. Pretend to be digging, or oiling a lathe. Maybe they won't notice you're still dressed like a hotel lock-out.

Air comes in jolting pockets, gulped into lungs filled only with the hope that this might be the last breath to come. I begin to twitch, to obsess, to fall into patterns so ingrained they have their own postcode. My muscles ache with the stress of prolonged clenching; readying to spring into flight the minute that fight loses out. The familiar pull of panic clutches at my chest, preparing to throttle every ounce of my resolve. Not now. Please not now.

You can't do this, it screams; echoing so loudly around my frenzied head I'm sure the room will hear. Run. Hide. Die. You will never survive this.

I grit my teeth and drop the robe.

PART ONE
THE ANXIETY

CHAPTER 1

ADVENTURES IN ANXIETY

Hello. I'm Paula and I'm anxious.

If you had managed to meet me at any point during my first three decades on this planet, that's pretty much the only thing I'd have been able to tell you about myself. Possibly not quite so 12-step succinctly, but the gist would have been the same, if you were close enough to catch it.

Of course, you never would have been close enough, unless you had found your way into my home, dragged me from under my blanket, and stopped me crying long enough to explain you only wanted to hear a little more about me. And, even then, faced with such a kindly house-breaker, I still probably wouldn't have had the nerve to say a word.

This is basically my rather inarticulate way of saying that, for most of my life, all I really knew about my own character was anxiety. Everything I was, any future I could have imagined, was tied to this most misleading of facts: I'm Paula and I'm anxious.

Back then, anxiety, in all its encompassing forms and fashions, was my constant. Every morning, every night, every in-between was coloured by its shadow and shaped by its trembling hand. Even on the best of days – and there were some, I promise – my fragile mental health had to be factored into plans made and situations arising, to the power of 10. Why 10? Because anything less would have been ineffectual, anything more might have been - gasp - noticed by lookers-on. And God knows, even my metaphors had to comply with generally accepted standards of decency.

I say "back then", as though describing a lifetime ago, when biscuits were bigger and my head was full of their broken bits. In some ways, I suppose, it was. The only reason I can share this with you now is because I'm thankfully more removed from its subject than I ever believed I could be. In other ways though, barely moments have passed, and I still wouldn't declare myself divorced from my past: separated, perhaps, but still bearing its name. Fortunately though, I like a good laugh, and if the finger of fun is pointed in my direction, all the better for everyone.

Before the words run away with me, I should tell you a little more about what you're getting yourself into by joining me between these inked pages. I won't lie, because I'm not paid any extra for it, but, at times, this isn't the happiest of stories. Cross Bambi with a D'Urberville and you won't go far wrong. That's the reality of mental ill health and, for me, it was the reality of life for long enough. But that doesn't mean you've signed up for a misery manual. If there's one decent thing about suffering chronic social anxiety, it's that matters so often go pear-shaped that you learn to press your own cider. And while it's not all comedy gold, hopefully there's enough silver in there to line the clouds I'm sharing.

Looking back, it's easier to spot distinct decisions and circumstances that kicked me onto the outlier's path, but my world was so mired in fear and obsession that I couldn't have seen crazy with a monocle and a tinfoil trilby. That's the other thing, I'll be using the C-word as and when it needs saying. I'm a proud crazy person with no need to flinch from wayward terminology: basket case, mental, nut-job, loon ball. They're me; they're mine. And while I own the words, they can never again be the master of me.

There it is then, social anxiety: the condition that defined almost 30 years of my existence without ever needing a dictionary. Broadly, an overwhelming fear of social situations, shared interactions, and the judgement of others. Narrowly, persistent grinding doubt and clawing worry, which eventually reduced me to a state not unlike your average landslide. The fun starts here, eh?

As anyone who has it knows though, social anxiety doesn't come alone. Hell, no! It drags the whole clan into town for the occasion. Panic attacks, depression, generalised anxiety disorder, addiction: uniting to take up so much room in a head that Environmental Health could start a file. And I had all of them: every confidence-shattering, strength-sucking, self-crushing one. While my teenage peers were imagining exactly which *Friends* character they would adult into, I was struggling to picture a grown-up version of myself able to spend time regularly with five other people, no matter how bright the colour palette and trend-setting the haircuts.

All I knew was that nothing was the same for me; not how I thought or what I experienced, and certainly not how I felt about the person I was becoming. It never had been and perhaps never would be either. I'm not sure I even recognised why for the longest of times, although the increasing medical intervention and countless appointments should have been an indicator. Actually, I probably could count them, if I really tried; I didn't complete an accounting degree for nothing.

Like boiling a frog, ever so gradually, anxiety singed my psyche, until I could no more separate its heat from my own. In the end, I wasn't even particularly unhappy, despite being almost 30, with more tics than a Lyme Disease ward, and unable to leave the house on my own without enough pills to numb a small nation. I just wasn't anything really. There was no longer room for emotion, never time to dwell or aspire. All there was, all there ever would be, was anxiety. The coping, the struggling, and, most importantly, the hiding of it.

Day by ordinary day.

AN ORDINARY DAY

Tuesday

3.14am

Sleep, goddammit.

I screw my eyes shut tightly and push them into the pillowcase with possibly too much force, but still they twitch open every second or so; eyelashes dragging against the white cotton below. Open, shut, open, shut. It's almost a routine now, this twice-nightly tango with tiredness – although I'd rather dance to any other tune.

Already my head begins to fill with life's nonsense; yesterday's mistakes and tomorrow's concerns. It's relentless and exhausting. But clearly not exhausting enough.

8.02am

I drop two more painkillers into an already mottled glass. The last two took the edge off, but there are three more edges still to battle. I've only been officially awake for 40 minutes and I'm almost losing count of the prescription-strength pills entering my system. What's another few when this dog has hair to spare? I make a note to find a new chemist on the commute; one that doesn't recognise me for what I am – yet.

The mirror glances at me on my way past, but I don't catch its eye. My reflection is just one more thing that I can no longer face. I hate her, that terrified woman in the glass, with the washed-out skin and broken stare. I can't look at her. I won't. At least this way I can deny knowing her.

My hand hovers over the door handle, waiting for my husband, Gerry, to urge its opening. Every morning, the same. I have to leave. I have a job, with colleagues who don't know of my difficulties, and won't ever, if I can just keep going. That's the beauty of social anxiety: I'm so worried what others will think if I don't act normally that I cause myself to act completely abnormally, just so I look normal. It's the reason I'm still forcing myself out to work every day, even though it's slowly, quietly killing me.

Gerry edges me gently onwards, outwards. I'm not agoraphobic, by any description. I love the outdoors; the expanse of nature calms my tiny soul. I'd climb a tree and bask a century among its branches; you know, if I could climb trees. There are just so many more people out here than in my two-bedroom flat. So many more chances to embarrass myself. To fail.

10.34am

I can't believe I just did that. Did they notice, those strangers with eyes, that might have been looking when I did that? Did they see? Should I just leave? I can't leave, I'm working. And besides, won't it be obvious if I move now? I should apologise. But I can't. Not to people I don't know, who don't know that I know that they saw, or heard, or didn't. It was nothing: an accidental slip, a word misplaced, an arm nudged. Maybe it was less than that, maybe more. I'm not sure I know now. Here it comes anyway. My face flushes first, my arms frozen to my sides. I'm sure they would see me trembling, if only they weren't already looking away in disgust. Or maybe, hopefully, disinterest. Can they even see me in this corner from there? I'm sure they're edging out. My heart beats a drum solo through my ribcage. Panic comes in floods, washing away my breath.

The wall reaches out to take my weight. If only the world had a trap door.

11.15am

Rain slaps my cheek. I deserve it, I'm sure. But I'm also grateful for its icy nails to cool this scene. The attacks take every ounce of me to control, even 15 years on from the first. I guess they've grown with me, like every faithful companion. I slam the car door. An act of frustration that never draws attention; one I can allow myself. My head rests on the steering wheel, where I'm sure its imprint is starting to show. I hope to God my workmates think I'm having an early menopause. Something medical, something understandable, something for which I don't need to be sorry. I left a note. A note of apology. Why did I leave an apology note? Again.

12.02pm

Turning the key, the engine starts; a local radio station's news bulletin blaring suddenly through the dusty speakers. Crap, not now. My hand grabs at the volume knob, quickly, fumbling it downwards until the presenter's clipped tones fall below human hearing.

A car bomb, killing eight people. The fragment of information I snatched from my sanity's control tells me all I need for the next spiral of guilt and fear. Anxiety sharpens emotion, until every problem, every concern is felt like a blade to the skull. Somehow, without my consent, this is all my doing and all mine to resolve. I just don't know how. I should be helping more, giving more, but I can't feel any more. I already feel everything, every second.

I try to avoid news now, on my worst days, as terrible as that seems. This way I only beat myself up for my own ignorance and selfishness, rather than all the world's failings. It's a little easier, but not much.

Looking around, I realise again that I'm parked on a busy road. Not a passer-by has glanced through my windscreen, but I still can't stay here, not for what I need to do next. I could just not bother, my brain tries to convince me, but I know better. The cereal bar tucked in my handbag isn't going to eat itself – unfortunately. And years of battling back to even just this level of fuelling my body means I understand how important those few calories I allow really are.

I edge into the traffic and turn up the next side street, careful to park directly behind another car, all the better to hide from view. It's not exactly the lunch of champions but, since I'm barely a challenger, the chocolate chip and oat melange will see me through. One bite in and that part of our evolutionary make-up that used to warn of oncoming wolves clocks an elderly gent on my nearside. I wait a beat, try to scrabble a scrap of reason from the mushrooming cloud. But where there's one person, it's public, and I don't eat in public.

I drop the cereal bar into the passenger foot-well.

Lunchtime is over.

1.22pm

The chemist calls from the back store: something about three-day usage. Yes, I say, shuffling out with my shame in a paper bag. It's been two years.

2.04pm

The phone rings. As usual, I let it go to voicemail, buying time with unearned pennies. I recognise the number, and I know what the chat will be about. But even though I'm pretty sure I could have this regular conversation without so much as a taxing thought, I don't feel able to just answer my friend's calls any more. I'll ring her back, of course, in an hour or so, when I've prepared how the chat might go. And after I've considered what she might ask, or the turns we could take, I'll be ready with my answers, without need for uncertainty.

The topic of the day isn't exactly my favourite on which to dwell anyway. The impending party; the event that everyone else is willing ever closer, but that I'm pulling back from quicker than it's coming. Three weeks away, give or take a blackout or two, and I'm losing more than sleep over its promise. Short of dying outright – and I'm short of most things – I can't avoid this one. They know all my tricks, every excuse: the three-day migraine run-up, the sick relative who might not hold on. Sure, I could tell them I'm struggling; that every second spent in their company feels like a plastic bag is being wrapped ever more tightly around my head. But that would mean admitting I'm not normal, and risking people – gulp – talking about me.

I can't imagine anything worse. Although actually, considering going to the party comes close.

4.52pm

I salute the solitary magpie as it watches me scuttle through the car park. One for sorrow. I don't believe the superstitions, necessarily, but it's easier not to have another potential repercussion on the agenda. Afternoon, Mr Magpie.

As days go, this one has surely gone. Not worse than any other, if you're keeping score, just the same. The same steady assault of situations I can't withstand. The same fleeting periods of solitary calm – locked in toilet stalls or loitering on empty stairwells.

My head hurts, always. Not long until respite now. Just one more stop. The bag of clothes still clutters up the car boot, since our clear-out of several weeks before. Mostly brand new, with tags attached; my inability to either use shop changing rooms or return ill-fitting items makes for quite a cluttered wardrobe. Today though, I'll do what I didn't manage yesterday, nor the day before, and drop the donation off to one of the 3,000 charity shops along the short commute. I've already driven by six, but I reckon they looked closed. And I'm sure that one only stocks furniture. There's a nice shop just a bit further along, with a space just outside that I can pull into, if it isn't taken. I don't like the look of the next few ... No, not again. I'm doing this right now. I will end this bloody day with a trickle of pride. There's one. Stop now. Right now. Do it.

I yank the wheel left before the fear can catch up, take the key from the ignition, and pause, rehearsing the interaction in all its likely permutations. They won't refuse the donation, surely. Can they even do that? I plan an apologetic response, just in case. Checking the route, I notice the small step up to the entrance, and make a note not to miss it. I think the door opens inwards, but it's hard to tell from here.

One more minute. Just one.

I can hear it happening. The shutter clatters towards the wet pavement.

The shop shuts for the night.

5.14pm

Home. I close the door.

And breathe.

I survived. Time to start thinking about tomorrow.

THE STORY

You know how when you hear a story often enough you start to believe it's actually true, even though logic tells you it wouldn't pass a lie detector test with a resting heart rate and a fake moustache? Like that one every kid shared as fact about the killer clowns waiting, at the school gates, to rip our innocent faces into smiling horrors. I'm pretty sure the tale was based on childish mischief and artificial flavourings, yet every year it came back, with the same authority as before. And we all kept telling it, so true it remained.

Well, that's just how my story began. Not in the playground, whispered from ear to unwashed ear, but told as truth and passed along, until it was all I knew about myself.

Paula is the shy one. The bookish one.

Paula is a little nervous. A lot nervous.

Paula prefers her own company.

Paula is anxious.

The trouble is it really was all true. In the moment it was said, with the intent with which it was spoken, it was the best way I could be described. Maybe the only way. I did act shy. I do love books. I often feel nervous. And my own company's alright, on a good day. But that's not the whole story – and for too long a time I believed that it was. So I grew, from a timid child, who spent much of her childhood hiding behind her older sister, to a fragile teenager, filled with self-loathing and tortured for it, and onwards, to the twitching, cowering, frightened adult I became. All the while, telling myself that same story. This is who I am; I can't change that. Anxiety was as much a part of me as was the gap between my teeth, but no trip to the orthodontist would ever be able to fix it.

By my late twenties, the story was my reality. In spite of the regular medical input, intermittent counselling, and obsessive research, more than two decades of believing that anxiety was my personality had made it so. I couldn't cure my own character; I just needed to learn to live with it, the way others live with a bad temper or jealous streak. Prescriptions could keep me as level as this pothole was ever going to be, and for the rest, I would manage the environment to best suit my disposition. Of course, none of this was particularly considered. If you're imagining a sit-down session with a flipchart and formulae, you're giving me more credit than my account deserves. There was no thought process, no progression; my coping strategies just developed out of necessity in any given situation. Life simply went on, and me with it. As new circumstances arose, I found my way through, normally by adjusting the plan and my dosage. Then, inevitably, I just wouldn't go back. Narrowing the world in this way seemed like my best option. I couldn't change my anxious nature so the only way through life was to go around it. The more I applied this method though, the harder it was to stop. If an experience caused me anxiety, all I could do was avoid it the next time, reinforcing the belief that I wasn't able to cope with even the most basic of human events.

Gradually, and without my attention, I became so sensitive to the symptoms of stress that, instead of just the unknown, I was cutting back on even the known quantities – and plenty of them. Visits to friends' houses, cinema trips, family phone calls: at the first sign of upset, they were gone, without consideration, without return. In the end, comfort could only be found in one specific zone: at home.

There were days when I just wouldn't leave, and only the overwhelming fear of people remarking on my absence prevented those days from turning to years, or forever.

Never once did I stop to question the status I'd given anxiety or think to demote it back to what it actually is: a mental health condition I had been suffering since before I could spell its name.

In spite of this, I'd reached out to everyone, everything that might be able to cushion my head from its own blows. Snake oil? Magic beans? Sure, I'll give that a go. Just tell me where to stick them. Anything to convince myself that I was at least trying. Obviously, nothing worked; how could it? No one could change the very nature of me. I was resigned to who I was and, slowly but with every certainty, the universe was coming to the same conclusion. By the time I'd exhausted all the professionals and "unprofessionals" alike, everyone was tired, and I was no further forward. I'm afraid we can't help you any more. There's nothing else we can do. This might just be as good as it gets for you.

This story of mine had but two endings in sight. Both involved hospital. I would stay there indefinitely, or I wouldn't stay alive. Either way, no sequel would be required. Then I began to change the narrative ...

Stories are our way of organising our surroundings, of making a little sense out of all the nonsense around us. We all tell them naturally, about ourselves and others, and mine, for 30 years, had only one plot point.

What we so often forget is that stories can change. All we have to do is start to question them.

QUESTIONS I'M OFTEN ASKED ABOUT ANXIETY – AND MY HONEST ANSWERS

Q. What on earth are you frightened of?

A. You. Well, not you specifically. But people like you. People, in general, really. Are you people? Then, yes, actually, you.

Q. What can I do for my friend / family member who is struggling with anxiety?

A. Firstly, thank you so much for caring about someone who suffers with anxiety. I know we're hard work, but we really don't mean it. Life really is as difficult for us as we make it seem, and we're sorry we make it hard for you too. Helping a person with anxiety looks different in every circumstance but giving us more time than you ever imagine necessary is normally a good start. Listen to us longer than you want to, encourage us to talk more than we deserve, and be there when everyone else has found their way out. And even though "must try harder" has become the tune to which my recovery dances, please never say these words to your loved one. Trust me, if they could try any harder, they would. And they will, with your support and hand to hold.

Q. Why don't you just stop worrying?

A. Why don't you just walk off that sore leg? Or let go of your constipation. Oh, you can't, it's a condition? Yeah, same.

Q. Are you more afraid in crowds than just sitting here with me?

A. Absolutely not. Crowds are wonderful, homogeneous beasts, in which I've always been able to disappear from sight and thought. No one judges the one in the crowd or expects anything from them. They're too busy enjoying being part of something bigger than themselves. Here, with you, I'm 50 per cent of the populace. And I'm not sure I can live up to those proportions.

Q. Are you flirting with me?

A. Probably not. I blink a lot. It's a nervous twitch. But I'm sure you're lovely.

Q. How did you cure your anxiety?

A. I didn't. I can't imagine I ever will. Anxiety doesn't just leave, sadly. No matter how many doors you show it, the damn thing never seems to find the handle. It clings on to every last fracture in the mind, ready to push apart the sides of even the slightest crack.

I still deal with anxiety every day. The only difference now is that I recognise it for what it is: just a tiny part of my overall make-up. The blusher, if you like, and I'm not planning to let a red face control the rest of my days.

Anxiety isn't my fault, it isn't my personality, and it certainly isn't my master. It's a disorder with which I suffered for far too long; and now it has to suffer me instead.

Q. Were you abused as a child?

A. No. I had a wonderful childhood, and have an incredible family. Anxiety can be triggered by many things, and it's understandable that people want me to point directly to the cause of my own, but I'm afraid there's no single event in my past that drove me to suffer anxiety so deeply. There were many different, complex elements of my personality and experience, on which anxiety fed mercilessly, and I'll tell you all about them. I promise I will – just not in one sentence.

Q. Does it make you nervous when I do this? Or that? [DOES THIS. THEN DOES THAT.]

A. Yes. Yes, it does.

Q. How did you manage to keep a job / get married / have friends if your mental health was really that bad?

A. Social anxiety is the world's least entertaining circus act. For as long as I can remember, I was juggling the fear of being among people with the fear of being judged for not being among them.

At the near-height of my hell, I was what I unapologetically call a functioning recluse. With the help of far too much medication and some truly bizarre coping mechanisms, I could just about manage to fashion an existence from the broken bits of my world. On good days, I could drag myself out to work, smile almost naturally, and resemble a human, before collapsing into bed, worn out from the everyday effort. From afar, I probably held together in a recognisable adult shape. Up close, I was clothes on a catastrophe.

Hiding social anxiety is a skill I learnt while my childhood pals were still taking recorder lessons. I became good at it because I had to. And living an outwardly normal life was just another part of that – milestones and all.

Q. Do you really hate people then?

A. Of course not. Here's the thing ...

THE SOCIAL ANXIETY TRAP

I love people. I always have. I love them with every fibre of my being – and I eat a lot of bran. I want them to thrive and succeed. I want them to smile and make merry. I want them to be free to be their wonderful, intoxicating selves. More than anything though, I really, really want them to love me too. I'll settle for like, but only the strong stuff.

There's my problem though. Well, one of them. I was always so scared that you wouldn't like me if I put a foot wrong that I would never risk walking towards you. If you didn't see what a bumbling fool I was, you'd have no reason to imagine I was one. Smart, right? The more I stayed away though, so as not to gamble with our potential friendship, the more difficult it became to move any closer. My social skills wouldn't stretch the distance I was putting between us, and eventually the chance would snap clean.

Social anxiety heightens that innate desire to be part of the pack; not the king or queen, just somewhere in the middle of the deck, a nice seven of hearts on which no one puts any pressure, other than to just be there, after six, doing its basic seveny thing. With the same breath, anxiety reminds you that the rest of the pack are so much more useful, that they don't really need you around. Five and two have got your shift covered, after all.

This very mind game tied my orbitofrontal cortex in big gooey knots for many a lonely season. You see, developing social skills isn't automatic, and I just never seemed to be in the right gear. No matter how many icebreakers found their way into my arsenal, I didn't quite have the gumption to hammer them home. The moment would pass and, with it, my chance to learn the lesson it might have taught, so that the next time, and the next, I'd be less inclined to even think of trying. That's the trap.

I was caught very young, but, oh, how I wanted to be free.

CHAPTER 2

ADVENTURES IN SHORT TROUSERS

When this story starts, at some shoulder-padded time in the eighties, childhood anxiety wasn't a thing. At least, in the east end of Glasgow, where illness only counted if it took a limb overnight, mental health problems were akin to scabies: everyone knew they existed but no one looked too closely for fear they might be catching. In an area where life expectancy could be measured in centimetres, and white collars were reserved for priests, health concerns extended only as far as the eye could see – with or without prescription specs.

Remember those black-and-white photos you see of kids with smudged faces and no shoes, playing happily with sticks on cobbled streets? We were their next generation: another arm-pull up the greasy pole, and with the well-scrubbed hands to prove it. Every ounce of class our community had was working; everyone wanting more for us than they ever had. Our city was given a bad press, for good reason and none, particularly the deprived east, where knife crime and gang violence were town mottos, were the papers to be believed. All I ever knew of its influence though was a sort of gruff kindness, borne out by the Hogmanay trips around the neighbours' smoke-filled flats to tell jokes for pocket money and shortbread rounds.

While I know that it's as cheesy as a goat's udder to say this, we were happy. There were troubles, of course, like the time my dad's face was slashed by a group of boys, as he tried to buy wine for my mum for their anniversary, and his blood marked a trail home in the freshly fallen snow. For the most part though, I was always well aware that my romper-suit pockets were filled with four-leaf clovers, my booties lined with the whitest of heather. Still though, how I fretted.

Imagine that you're five years old – aww, you are cute! – and, although your belly is full and your hands are held, something, everything, is worrying you. You begin to twitch, your eyes are blinking so much there's a headwind. It's not right, of course, but you've never known anything different, so you don't think to bring it up. In school, your eyes, and teeth, and hair are checked, your intellect examined, and your resolve tested. But never your head health. Surely if it was important, they'd test that too.

Besides, it's just your nature to feel like this. Everyone says so. And every other trait of your developing personality points that way, or at least gesticulates in its general direction.

Super-sensitive

I don't know what the rest of you were doing for feelings in the eighties, because I was definitely using up all the emotions on offer. Even as an infant, I felt the world's problems and failings like everyone belonged to me. By the age of five, I wanted to adopt kids, as I just couldn't imagine anyone not having a family – and I had enough love to go around. My heart hurt for everyone, and my head found places to carry you all around. I'd like to say it was acute empathy but then I'd like to say I was a cute empath too, and there's no evidence for either.

Not only human people found their way under my sensitive skin though. I would shuffle milk cartons closer together in supermarkets, in order that they weren't lonely, let midges bite me if they really needed the blood, and hold tiny funeral services for lost bugs.

I'm using the past tense only for effect, you realise. I still love a milk carton couple.

Careless

Not with things, you understand, since things were important, but I was always fairly careless with myself. Clumsy, to the extreme, with no real spatial awareness, I never quite found my way through an afternoon completely uninjured. Despite being so exceptionally timid, I often wandered into situations that I'm pretty sure weren't as safe as I somehow perceived. I recognise now, of course, that I just didn't have any context for fear, given that everything was equally terrifying for young Paula. One Christmas, I ran back into my burning primary school, with fire alarm blaring and teachers clamouring, to collect the Bananarama cassette a friend had given me as a present that morning.

Like I said, careless.

Introverted

To say I liked my own company as a child would probably be reductive, since I only really appreciated it in comparison to anyone else's. Not that I didn't like the company of others; it was more that I just couldn't relax until I was alone, or in my own small family group once more. At parties or gatherings, while my sister was holding court, I was holding out for the promise of bedtime surely soon to come. The routine was automatic – smile, admit that, yes, I was probably taller than last time, step behind my sister Donna, and move slowly towards the door. It worked for almost 30 years.

Timid

You've heard of Snow White's sidekick, Bashful? Yeah, he was my gregarious pal. It would be fair to say that I wasn't the most outgoing of children, mainly because I didn't really like going out. Or staying in, really, if there were other folk around. I was fine, mostly, as long as no one asked me a question, or looked vaguely in my direction, or said my name, or drew attention to the fact that I was around. So mostly not fine then.

I couldn't bear voices raised even a decibel above lullaby levels. I can still quite easily conjure the sound of my very screechy first teacher, if ever I have the need to induce terror deep in my very soul. I'll admit, I've yet to find a practical use for the skill.

Bookish

I've always had a decent enough brain. We're not the greatest of allies at times, but I recognise her quality, particularly when she thinks our way out of a mess I've landed us in. Sharp, astute, intuitive: I was already able to read on starting school at four and a half, and quickly rose through the ranks of teacher's pet all the way up to brown-nose. But my sense, such as it is, has always verged towards the uncommon. Hand me a screwdriver and you'll watch me drive a screw mad before I ever manage to fix anything. While friends skipped or rode bikes, I wrapped myself in their discarded jumpers to sit on the cold stairwell and write bad poetry.

And, by God, have I always loved books. I come from the kind of family that reads first, does later. Later usually comes after just a few more chapters. Dog-earing makes me madder than a riled Rottweiler. My favourite game as a kid was Library, in which my sister and I would arrange our piles of books into categories in our tenement hallway, and the other kids in the street could borrow them, as long as they printed their names on the log sheet and returned them by the date penned on our handmade dust-jacket inserts. My sister was front of house; I was librarian.

Hopeful

I was going to change the world. All those problems that disturbed my every sleep, they could be fixed: I just wasn't big enough yet to fix them. But one day I would be.

As a little person, even the optimism in me was defined by my desire to make the things better that caused me such incomprehensible distress.

As a little person still, barely treble the height I've ever been, I now understand that this was just my way of managing those feelings of impotence. I couldn't control the anxiety I felt, but maybe, just maybe, in time I could contain its source. Plus, I really did want to change the world.

Don't get me wrong though – if it sounds like my wellbeing wasn't important to those around me, I'm not making the right kind of noises. Our home was filled with music and giggles and enthusiastic Scrabble contests. I painted rainbows on the skirting boards and there they stayed. We made dens from bed sheets and kitchen chairs. And I was cared for more than I probably ever deserved to be.

I still remember the doctor's appointments, as my parents noticed my blinking was steadily worsening. The trips to the optician to make sure my sight wasn't the issue. The referral to that crackpot consultant.* Anything that could be done to find the cause, or the cure for whatever was ailing me. In all those consultations, no one ever mentioned anxiety. I'm certain that if they had, my folks would have learnt all that the eighties could teach them of the condition. If you knew my family, you would understand.

Wait, let me introduce you ...

* The consultant in question was a paediatric specialist with all the bedside manner of a wildcat. One 20-minute appointment with him left me wary of hospitals and jowls for my entire childhood. In fact, just hold on a few more pages and I'll come back to him.

THE CAST

Main characters:

Name: Rose.

Relationship: Mother.

Personality: Warm, resilient, with the kind of patience that saints envy. Slow to anger, quick to forgive, and scared of absolutely nothing. Possesses a temper so even you could skate it. Only ever raises her voice to cheer us on. Adventurous in spirit and in action; definitely the doer of the family. Busy – like a bee but minus the sting – with an industrious nature and a practical skill-set. Never, ever tires of being exactly where she is needed, no matter how far she has to go. Fun to be around; an incredible friend. The kind of parent with which every human being should be blessed.

Name: Eric.

Relationship: Father.

Personality: Confident and genial, but with mood swings you could loop the loop on. An honest-to-goodness Glasgow gent: likes a pint but never swears in front of a lady. Knows everyone in the city; making him incredibly time-consuming to walk anywhere alongside. A pacifist, both through choice and lack of combat skills. Lost two and a half fingers in a work accident; calls the remainder his "wee hand". Taught me to be a free and open thinker. Emotional – has been known to shed tears at particularly poignant *Flintstones* episodes – but completely comfortable displaying it. Has told us he loves us every day of our lives.

Name: Donna (nickname: Dubbidy – I struggled to pronounce Donna for a while. It was an irritating time for everyone.)

Relationship: Older sister.

Personality: Friendly, dynamic, full of chat. Self-assured and a natural athlete; popular among her peers. Quick-tempered and scary when angered, but with a heart as squidgy as they come. Helpful to a fault; unfortunately, that fault is that she's so full of help she sometimes forgets to ask whether or not you need it. Fiercely protective of her frightened sibling: once chased and caught a notorious bully and clouted him with his own school bag. Easy to wind up, if you know where the crank handle is; little sisters always know.

Name: Catherine.

Relationship: Gran.

Personality: Strong, stoical, enduring: a constant in my early life. Introduced me to sugar in my tea and the joy of watching snooker on a black-and-white telly: the blue ball was the one behind the green. Loved a game of cards and would happily cheat us out of our pocket money, only to buy us whatever we wanted anyway. Always teaching us; even, in the end, about true loss.

Supporting cast:

Extended family: When your mother is one of eight siblings and your father one of 10, your family tree begins to resemble more of an orchard. Being the youngest member of the clan meant a million weddings, being spoilt rotten by aunts and uncles at the seaside, and Christmases surrounded by tipsy cousins that you kinda fancied and weren't sure if you were allowed to or not. There was always someone to be visiting, always a kettle on, and always so many thank-you phone calls to be too shy to make every birthday.

Friends: Whether by geographical or societal happenstance, there were always other kids around throughout my youth. School friends who recognised that my idea of playtime was just to move my books outside; local pals whose families felt like my own, given the amount of time I spent in their homes. For all my quirks and oddities, other children didn't really seem to notice – or at least didn't particularly care. To them, I was just Paula, who didn't like sport and cried a bit more than they would have expected. Sure, my twitches sparked curiosity aplenty, but the doctors would soon sort that out.

THAT CRACKPOT CONSULTANT

Take a seat.

Mum leads me towards one of two plastic chairs in the small hospital office. The room smells funny: like when our downstairs neighbour washes the stairs with too much soap. I perch on the edge, reach for Mum's hand, as she settles into position beside me. She helps me out of my jacket. The doctor hasn't looked up from the folder on his big, messy desk.

I've never met him before; he's not the usual one we visit, with the kind smile and silly questions. This one looks strict. He makes me think of a Roald Dahl character, with untidy tufts of hair poking from behind big ears, and skin falling in flaps from a puffy face. Little round glasses sit on the end of his nose. I wonder why they don't slip right off when he nods, which he does a lot as he reads. He's old, like Gran, but not in a jolly way. I bet he doesn't play cards like her either. I grip Mum's hand tighter as they start to talk.

La, la, la, I try not to listen. I don't want to hear what the grown-ups are saying this time. They're talking about my stupid eyes. I don't know why they blink so much, but I don't think they're meant to, because everyone looks at them funny when they do. And even I know you're not meant to blink when your eyes are closed. But I can't help it; I have to do it. When people notice, it makes it worse. It hurts when they go this fast. They don't even close at the same time, so sometimes I look like I'm winking, then I have to even them up by closing the other one, and ... it makes me very tired.

The doctor moves around the desk until he's almost next to me. He hasn't stood up, he's just wheeling his chair around on the bumpy brown carpet. He's still asking questions but they're not for me. I'm glad. My tummy is flipping upside down and my head is sore, and I couldn't sleep last night so I just want to stay quiet. He's putting something cold in my ear and muttering. But I can't hear him really because he's putting something cold in my ear. I want to remind him it's my eyes we're here for, but I think that would be rude, so I don't. He looks into my mouth too; at least I know he can't ask me to talk just now.

My whole face feels like it's moving now, but I'm not telling it to. My cheek scrunches up as if half of my face is smiling. I don't feel like smiling. I wish we could go home. But it's my turn to answer questions now. The doctor is looking at me.

Do you read?

Yes.

I nod. I like this question; I know how to talk about books.

What do you read?

He's back behind his desk now, staring at me over the top of his glasses. He's tapping a silver pen against the arm of his chair. Tap. Tap. Tap.

Anything.

I whisper the word because I'm still scared but I know he hears me because he looks different now; like he's laughing at me, but not happy. When he speaks again his voice is loud and his chins wobble.

'Anything? French, German, SPANISH?!'

I hold my breath. He's really angry but I don't know what I've done wrong. I can feel tears coming but I know everything will be okay when Mum leans forwards. She uses her other voice – the one I only ever hear when she's talking to someone silly.

'She's five. She means anything in English, obviously.'

That is what I meant, of course. I thought he would know that though, since he's a doctor and they're clever people. I'm really embarrassed now; I didn't explain it properly. No wonder he's mad. Mum wraps her arm around my shoulders and I cuddle in to her side. She wipes a tear from the end of my nose. The doctor watches, writes something down in scribbles. He doesn't look up for his next question.

Why are you crying? What is there to cry about?

I don't know the answer. I try to think but my brain is all muddled. This is how it gets sometimes; when people are around, when I don't know what to say. My head gets so busy, like all the thoughts are fighting each other, and I can't pick the right one out. I squeeze Mum's hand because I know she's getting ready to tell the doctor off and I don't want her to make a fuss. Please don't make a fuss. She sits back in her chair a little, but her teeth don't open when she answers, as if she's holding some words in.

'She's frightened. That's why she's crying.'

The doctor shrugs, shakes his head. I wish he would just say what's wrong with me. I'm sure he knows. It's so warm now and I don't think there's much air left – that's how it feels anyway. I pretend I'm somewhere else: with Dad and Donna at home, sitting on the living-room floor, playing Countdown.

But he doesn't let me stay there for long because he shouts, towards the open door.

'Nurse. Bring me one of the large syringes. The really big one.'

He holds up his hands to show the size, wider apart than I've ever seen a syringe fit. I hear myself sniffing, and my collar is wet where the tears have started to drip. I really, really don't want a jab that big. I'm sure it will hurt, and I'm already scared. I don't think the doctor will be kind either, not like the school nurse, who hides the needle behind her back so you don't see it coming.

He thumps his big hands on the table, pushes himself out of his seat a little bit.

'You think I'm going to give you a jab, don't you?' He smiles. 'Well, I'm not!'

He spits out the last word, and little bits of his mouth water hit my forehead.

Mum is already standing up. She pulls my jacket from the back of the chair, and I put my arms in like I know she wants me to. Her hand is in mine and we're at the door before I even remember walking.

'No, you are not. What kind of idiot are you, speaking to a child like that?' I hear him mumbling something about eye pressure, but the door slams shut behind us. I never, ever want to talk to a doctor again.

Diagnosis:

There is nothing wrong with this child. The excessive blinking is a habit, caused by a desire to mimic her mother.* No further treatment required.

AN EMBARRASSMENT OF TWITCHES

The story goes – and I have the scars to prove it – that I was 18 months old when everything changed. Hold up, before you start reminding me of my earlier assertion that there wasn't one single event in my childhood that triggered anxiety in me, I have to emphasise the point that there were many. Not that I had a youth plagued with misfortune; just a very hospitable head space in which anxiety could breed. Little things at which your eyelid would not bat, caused mine to whip up a gale. But this thing, well, this wasn't little. Or so I'm told.

I have no memory of the day I crawled to the bathroom, squeezed through the half-open door and knocked a cup of boiling water down upon myself. My parents though, they have all the memories: of hearing the cup topple from the unit, of the horror of my scream as it soaked through my pyjamas, of grabbing up my small body

* No one in my family twitches. Except if you throw something at their face. Trust me, I've tried.

and holding it under the cold tap until the ambulance arrived. And so followed the most horrendous few days for my family, as I was covered and uncovered in ointments and bandaging in an array of different hospital wards, and my folks were asked to go over again and again the worst thing that had ever happened to them. Was it really possible for this to have taken place in the 20 seconds my mother's eyes were on my sister? Of course, they had to check to make sure I hadn't been the victim of anything other than my own curiosity, but had clearly never met a toddler before ... In 20 seconds I could have brought down society, never mind just causing myself a mischief – albeit a serious one.

For months I lived in the burns unit, alongside fireworks victims and injured miners, who would take turns to walk me around the ward in my pram, strengthening their wounded legs and lulling me to sleep. My parents were forever by my side and eventually I was well enough to be back by theirs at home, with daily visits to the clinic for dressing changes. By luck – and the constraints of gravity – the water had left its mug and missed mine. Instead it landed squarely on my torso, then rounded off the corners. And due to my father literally saving my skin with his quick-thinking and quicker action, I wouldn't be scarred. Except that I am.

No, I'm not using a poignant metaphor for the emotional sores that remained, although I'm clearly setting this particular story down because I know it must have affected my mental health across the years. What I mean is that I really am physically scarred by the experience, since a poor student nurse was left alone to apply my various creams and accidentally slathered my blisters in the wrong medication. Thankfully I don't have to remember the initial pain, or months of ensuing treatment, but I'm often reminded of its legacy. Several decades on, my frontage still resembles a prune with ambition, making sunbathing impossible. And communal dressing rooms are the place where self-esteem goes to die. Sure, there's a long list of pretty obvious consequences of my scalding; I wrote it during an especially self-destructive period of adolescence. Body confidence issues, difficulty with upper body movement, and a lifelong phobia of large bodies of water: you don't need the Hubble telescope to spot the connection there. But the most debilitating effect of the accident for me wasn't quite so up-front.

Embarrassment, in all its flushed forms, is a natural bedfellow of social anxiety, and it's one that I was awakened to very early. I'm not sure when I first realised that my body wasn't quite how it should be, but the shame stuck with me like an abusive limpet. Year upon year, I suffered the ritual humiliation of baring my developing chest to a burns unit doctor, in case my growing body tore the damaged tissue and left me in need of a skin graft. I couldn't tell if the doctors were becoming more attractive or if I was just becoming more attracted, but, either way, by my 15th annual check-up, the level of teenage hormones in the room could have sparked a third Summer of Love.

I will never forget though, trying, with still shaking hands, to re-knot my school tie as medical professionals I'd never met quietly discussed my skin's impressive endurance, despite my apparent appetite to outgrow it. They had seen a thousand bodies, examined a million scars, but I couldn't shake the crushing embarrassment of exposing mine.

That kind of awkwardness elbows its way into your consciousness, spreads out and makes itself comfortable – while you're left feeling very much less comfortable. Joining forces with anxiety, it convinced me not only to be ashamed of what I was becoming, but to hide it, and deny the struggling for all I was worth. Luckily, I wasn't worth much.

THINGS I'VE BEEN LESS EMBARRASSED ABOUT THAN HAVING ANXIETY

- Failing my driving test five times.
- Having my first kiss in a bus stop with a man twice my age who smelt of onions.
- Catching head lice at the age of 19.
- Crying at a Take That concert because Robbie breathed the same room-air as me.
- Having half a bikini wax because, to continue the indignity, would have been frankly unbearable.
- Harbouring a lifelong crush on Michael Palin, to the point that we just had to go to his book signing during our honeymoon. I couldn't speak to him.
- Growing my own coat because I ate so little during my teenage years that my body sprouted lots of lovely hairs to keep itself warm. I'm basically a llama.
- Keeping head lice until the age of 20 rather than face another awkward visit to the local chemist.
- Piercing my own belly button and pretending to everyone it was done by a professional, even though it was lopsided and turned green.
- Falling so in love with a lecturer that I didn't submit the course assignment in case it ruined my chances.
- Spitting chewing gum into the face of a guy I really liked while just trying to reply to his casual greeting.
- Not showering for a fortnight because I felt bad for the bacteria.
- Failing my driving test the sixth time.
- And this ...

POTTING THE BROWN

Plop.

The tiny white ball drops into a corner pocket. I know this means it's my turn now, but Claire just takes it back out and keeps playing, and we're not really keeping scores anyway. Even though we're both small, we're hunched over the miniature snooker table on my bedroom floor, giggling as we hit all the wrong colours with the pencils we're using as cues. I think the real cues are in the cupboard but it's almost time for Claire to go home now, and I can't really be bothered looking for them. Claire accidentally bumps the table leg, and the balls all scatter again. It's the third time one of us has messed up the game. It doesn't matter. We've known each other since we were really little. She's nice; she's my friend.

But, right now, I really want her to leave.

My Scooby Doo clock says it's nearly three o'clock. Claire's mum should be back to pick her up soon. She already has her jacket on and we're waiting to hear the car horn beeping outside, but right now it's my turn at snooker and I have to crouch back down. Oh no. My tummy has been grumbling for ages. It was already feeling odd when Claire arrived, but once there are other people here in my house, there's nothing I can do. I've never been able to do any of that stuff outside of my own bathroom, and not ever when anyone is nearby. It's just too yucky and not nice, and makes me all embarrassed and ... I don't want to talk about it.

I miss all the balls on purpose, and sit back on the carpet, trying to listen to what Claire is saying but only hearing my own gurgling tummy and feeling my insides scrunching up again and again. I'm so worried and it's too warm in here now, even though it's freezing outside. I hope Claire can't see that I'm squirming, but I have to keep moving to stop things from happening. But they are happening, and I can't stop them.

Claire puts down her pencil cue and goes over to the window. I think she knows. I should just excuse myself, like Mum taught me, and go, but the toilet is only across the hall and I'm afraid Claire will hear and tell everyone at school. I'll have to just wait. I'll have to. But it hurts, and I don't know how to control what my body is doing, and I don't think I can hold it any longer. My muscles relax all of a sudden, without me telling them to. I think I'm going to ... no, no, no.

Plop.

I think I'm going to cry. I'm biting my lips and I know my cheeks are going really red. I still need to pee and I can't let that go too, so I'm still concentrating really hard. But the effort is too much. I just want to run away.

Claire's face has changed. Maybe she knows and doesn't want to say. I can't really move. Everything is sticking together inside my leggings, and I'm scared it'll all leak out. This is the worst thing ever. There's nothing I can do. Claire is talking but her voice is funny. I wonder if she's holding her breath. I'm holding mine. It's helping me hold what's going on inside, but mostly I really just don't want to smell anything. Not anything at all.

When I rock onto my side a bit to check the carpet isn't mucky, Claire doesn't laugh so maybe she hasn't noticed after all. But as soon as her mum's car toots downstairs, she rushes towards the door. I have to stand up. It's polite to walk your friends out. My leggings are heavy and I think they're bulging under my cardigan. They might fall down and everything splatter out, so I hold them with both hands at the waist. I can't walk fast. Claire already has the front door open and shouts goodbye as she leaves. I can hear Gran coming out from the kitchen to make sure we're okay. I shut the door quickly and run into the bathroom, breaths coming in and out all at once.

I clean myself up through the tears and throw my clothes in the bin when Gran isn't looking.

I'm six years old, and I'm a mess.

PUTTING CHILDHOOD TO BED

I love to sleep. It's my most favourite verb, with 'to prefer' coming in a close second. A day without a nap is a day that should end very early indeed – and normally does. I've always appreciated a good kip. As a baby, I was the kind of bundle of flesh that didn't particularly enjoy being awake, unless food was on the menu, and, even then, I often had to be woken up to be reminded I was hungry. There was nothing wrong with me or anything; I was just a dopey little sod.

In time, sleep became an escape from anxiety; the one place no one cared if my thoughts were completely crazy. In fact, it was absolutely expected. Intense nightmares, regular sleep-walking, bouts of insomnia, all threatened over the years to end our relationship, but once I'm back there, basking in its warm oblivion, sleep and I are the kind of friends that only exist in dreams.

Like anything precious though, sleep became a prize in my childhood; something to be coddled and protected, something that had to be done properly. Around the age of seven, I began to build a routine to prepare for sleep. Not a teeth brushed, face washed, kind of routine. That stuff was a given; I ain't no urchin. This was more like settling the questions of the daytime to make way for sleep's answers. Also, it was a little bit crazy.

Before long, the actions became a nightly ritual, taking on more meaning than was ever the intention. That one night I was too tired to go through the motions, sleep didn't come, or was fitful at best, adding ever more weight to the need to stick to the script. I never explained its importance, but soon it wasn't enough for me to be the only participant in the routine. After my own drill was done, one or other of my parents was then expected to replicate the procedure fully. I think they drew straws. Sometimes it took half an hour or more, and our eyes were crossing before we'd successfully dotted the Ts. I never slept over at other people's houses; I didn't have the energy to adapt the programme.

For three years, this was bedtime.

Step 1: Switch on big light.

Step 2: Check window is closed and locked, and key is removed from room.

Step 3: Shake curtain firmly and smooth down before closing. Repeat with second curtain. Ensure curtains meet exactly in middle of window – pin together if necessary.

Step 4: Open and shut wardrobe door once. Open again and ruffle through clothes. Close door securely. Step 5: Check under head of bed visually. Check under foot of bed visually. Step 6: Reach under head of bed and pat floor, patting slowly all the way to foot of bed. Continue patting back to head of bed.

Step 7: Announce clearly that there is nothing under bed. Step 8: Switch on lamp. Wait five seconds.

Step 9: Switch off big light. Step 10: Look under pillow for tissues. If none, find tissues, place under pillow. If room was exited, start process again from Step 1. Step 11: Touch outside of every electrical socket in room to ensure all are empty.

Step 12: Arrange 12 favourite teddy bears in an exact arc in bed, each in their own specific position in the line-up. Make sure duvet covers the entire gang, with no gaps for movement or draughts.

Step 13: Switch off lamp.

Goodnight, scary world.

CHAPTER 3

ADVENTURES IN ADOLESCENCE

You know how when you walk towards an automatic door and nothing happens? And it crosses your mind, just for an instant, that it might not have noticed you, that somehow you don't quite exist in its reality? And you hesitate, almost imperceptibly, a tiny falter in your step, before the door sweeps open for you to carry on with your day. You don't think about it again – it wasn't exactly a formative moment – but it knocked you, only briefly, off your stride.

Growing up, for me, was a continuous string of those moments, knotted around a brain that did not have the emotional breadth to cope with them. Perhaps it's the same for everyone. Let's face it, adolescence was only ever the best years of life in the 1800s, and that's because there was no pressure for anyone to actually survive them. Add 24/7 anxiety into the equation though and the mental maths become ever more messy.

Little things that others would walk off more easily than a footballing foul were like death blows to my fragile ego, cannoning into my self-esteem, chipping gradually away at its corners. I can still conjure up the scene in my mind of the first time I was called Blinky;

I know the smells and the sounds like they still cling to my senses. I can almost feel the grooved wooden desk that I gripped, as I steeled myself against the words. As hard as I've tried to forget it, I remember his name. I remember it all. 11 years old, still with the childish notion that life is fair, and I'd just found my way onto the bad kid's hit-list. Of course, that bad kid was probably dealing with a whole heap of hell in his own world but, as he opened his mouth to shout my new nickname across the Classical Studies room, all I could hear was the next five years of misery rushing towards me.

Blinky. Not exactly original, but insightful in its own way, I'm sure. I had only been in the school a matter of months and already it had started. If I had known then that the end wouldn't come until the very day I left, at 16, to start my undergraduate degree, maybe I would have tried to find another way out. As it was, I bowed my head to the slander and spittle, and hid from the growing pool of bullies. I'm more than a little proud of how adept I became at moving through an educational establishment unseen; attending church services in the school's makeshift chapel to avoid the lunchtime crowd, slinking through corridors in which, technically, pupils weren't allowed. But I was a good student – smart enough and with a genuine interest in learning – so some of the more punitive rules could bend, as long as I didn't snap them in others' faces. I reckon most of the teaching staff knew the gauntlet I was running every moment I was within school grounds. It still took years though, and I needed my sister to start the fight-back, before I'd admit anything was actually amiss. But amiss it very much was.

Once I was branded a target, naturally I became the butt of any wayward anger, since there was no point in aiming elsewhere. Whatever they were exorcising – insecurities, frustrations with schoolwork, difficult home lives – I was their vessel, and that demon would be kicked right out of me. At least sitting ducks have the option of flight; open season on this bird started in August and ended in July. With every turn of the summer arrived a fresh intake of hunters in the field; the babies of the high school, ready to prove themselves stronger and crueller than those that had gone before.

After a while, despite what I was told, names really did hurt me. And while they never did break my bones, I could tell you a few stories about the damage of sticks and stones ...

STICKS AND STONES

My only crime today is walking to school, the same way as every other day. That's enough, apparently, to merit a 20-minute stream of insults, ranging from the baffling to the downright obscene. What's a ratchet anyway? I'm pretty sure I wouldn't put one where they're suggesting.

Pathetic.

It's only Tuesday, and already I've had pasta from what can only have been an improvised Home Economics lesson in my hair, and sour milk over my brand-new skirt. When I take off my uniform most nights, Mum doesn't know if she's doing a washing or a stir fry. I've decided not to let such mindless abuse ruin another day though. They're not getting into my head any more.

I quicken my step again, since my head is better protected if it's slightly further away, and my friend does the same. We're both regularly forced to speed walk to class in the morning, although it's probably more like speed wandering the way I do it. The boys just pick up their own pace to keep up, but at least the whole sorry scenario reaches school faster. That reminds me, double Physics this afternoon; must remember to sit further from the Bunsen burners this time – hence the skirt replacement. I don't think I can get away with another lie about standing too close to a bonfire. It's February.

'Check the state of your ...'

I stop listening almost as soon as the new guy joins the party. I don't need to know the particular noun he's attacking: hair, clothes, face – his mates have pretty much covered the whole collection before he has even left the house. But still he tries to come up with something original about my person to rip apart. I can almost hear the bile bubbling in his mouth.

I turn my attention instead to our own bitty conversation about an upcoming gig we're hoping to persuade our families we just can't miss, but it's so hard to be enthusiastic when words like "disgusting" and "fat bitch" are being hurled in my direction. Why don't they ever miss?

I stop suddenly. Damn, I didn't mean to come this way. We should have turned at the main road, instead of taking our usual shortcut. I glance back, trying to calculate if we have time to double back before they reach the corner. We don't. They're barely a few footsteps behind us now and I know that, if I'm thinking this looks dangerous, it won't be long before they're thinking it too. I can't believe I forgot that the builders left a four-feet rubble heap at the kerbside. We were lucky on the way home yesterday, but luck doesn't last in these parts. I'm really glad the council is finally renovating those ugly old flats, but did they really need to leave a DIY weapons store on my already treacherous morning route?

We hurry on. Maybe if we can just get far enough past the pile, we'll be out of reach. But no, there it is. The cheer goes up as I can only imagine they spot the goodies. Who thinks like that? Who sees rubbish in the street as a way to make someone's life worse? It baffles me. But I get the feeling I won't be baffled for long.

It hits me square on the back of the head. I stumble forwards, trying to stay on my feet but not managing for long. My knees take a jolt as they thump down on the pavement. I've no idea if I'm bleeding; I don't have time right now to check. I can just about see and, as far as I can hear, I'm giving great comedy value. I'm being helped up hurriedly. I know we need to move but it's not coming easily. Bending to pick up my rucksack, I catch sight of the chunk of marble that just bounced off my skull. It's huge, and I'm actually kind of impressed that he managed to lob it so far.

I'm dizzy as we start walking again but stopping would be stupid. My eyes are watering or crying – maybe both – as we rush through the gates into the school yard. I feel sick and the pain is coming in floods, but we won't tell anyone; we never do. And the worst thing: the bell hasn't even gone yet, and they've already broken back into my head.

NOT SO JOLLY HOCKEY STICKS

I've never been the most practical of souls. Sure, I can change a light bulb, but only if it really wants to change. And, even then, I need a manual and a support group. Before the jokes begin to form themselves though, my gender has no bearing on my utter uselessness. In fact, I take after my dad in this particular respect. He wouldn't mind me saying that we share a complete ineptitude for all things beyond pure theory. We were once left to build a flat-pack shelving unit together and spent four hours making word puzzles from the instructions instead. Needless to say, Donna threw the shelves up in the ad break from *My So-Called Life* with her ingenuity, and a tool she made from lollipop sticks.

Of course, my dad is actually handless, or at least fingerless, since he lost half a high-five in an industrial accident years ago. My excuse? 45per cent clumsiness, 50per cent fear and 9per cent bad maths. I've never really understood how other people know what the extremities of their bodies are doing, minute to minute. If I'm scratching my knee, God knows what my elbow's doing, never mind anything on the other side of my shambling mass. My feet could be dancing a jig and I'd be none the wiser until the neighbours called up to complain. And don't talk to me about spatial awareness because I just don't know where you're coming from.

I could have practised, I guess; improved my hand–eye coordination so that the twain should never accidentally meet. Instead though, I accepted my ungainliness with quiet – and sometimes clattering – resignation, and avoided anything that could be construed as physical. Sports, games, outdoor pursuits; even knitting had to be practised in a corner under a blanket. I couldn't bear being watched trying anything new. Rather than an opportunity to learn and have fun, to me, these were only opportunities to fail – and with an audience. Very early on in life then, I began to shy away from new experiences. Anxiety latched on to that tendency, and soon I was convinced that not only was I rubbish at anything outside my current skill-set, but also that I should be terrified of trying to improve.

By the time I reached high school, P.E. was already a no-go. So far off the agenda that I'd go to any lengths to avoid the shame of each 50-minute fiasco. Leaving my kit in a hedge, adopting a tri-monthly menstrual cycle; I forged so many excusal notes that my mum had to change her signature. It didn't help, of course, that my sister was an athletic goddess and the teaching staff expected the second daughter of the family to have come off the manufacturing line in the same mould. Imagine their disappointment. Actually, you don't have to, since I can illustrate it with a simple story. One bright spring morning, I bumped into a P.E. teacher on the steps just outside the school building, and she reminded me that the annual sports day was taking place that week. Slightly scared that I was about to be asked to practise my egg-spooning, I stuttered back that I knew, and lied that it should be a good event. As I made to step past though, she said the words that defined my relationship with sport for decades to come: 'Just stay at home that day, Paula; we want your class to have a chance at winning.'

So I started to stay at home – not literally – I was the perfect attendance type, but I would no longer engage with anything that involved Lycra or lactic acid. I raked the sand of the long jump for a whole term of track and field, and opted for extra homework when given the choice, rather than embarrass myself on any court or pitch.

If they forced a hockey stick into my hand, I would lean on its edge by the sidelines, letting the ball trickle past without any effort to divert it. Soon, they stopped even counting me among the numbers. There's not a netball bib for Anxiety Attack.

In five years of secondary education, I managed to learn one thing about sport: that there was nothing I could learn from sport.

PANIC STATIONS

The girls' changing room is the usual commotion. There are bodies everywhere, crammed onto the slatted benches, in various states of undress. One of the older girls is loudly whispering the school's latest scandal to the rest of her clique, who shriek and gasp at all the expected moments. I've heard the word "cucumber" twice, and have no intention of listening for a third.

I've managed to squeeze my way into the usual corner, eyes to the floor so as not to catch the attention of any passing abuse. It's already been a difficult morning. Nothing beyond the usual jostling and jeering, but some days it's just harder to ignore than others. This is some days.

And now there's swimming. I'm sure there are worse places to be than here, but I'm struggling to imagine any, given that bodies of water terrify me. But before I'm even faced with that, I have to change from the protection of my bulky uniform into a one-piece horror show. Some of the more sporty girls have already somehow morphed into their costumes, breaking neither sweat, nor stride in the process. With one leg in, and one leg out of my tights, I'm teetering on the edge of social collapse, when my chest starts to tighten – really tighten. I've felt this sensation before, but never this much. If I hadn't looked down twice now, I'd believe that I'm being held in some sort of weird wrestling move, but no one is touching me. So why do I feel like my ribcage is in a vice?

I ... can't ... breathe.

There's no air in here. No one else seems to notice. They're still chatting but the sound isn't reaching my ears because THERE'S NO AIR. It's like that time ... no, that other time ... with the thing and those people ... oh God, why can't I think ... just calm down, calm the hell down ...

I'm going to die.

Every thought I've ever had is coming to the surface now. They're telling me I'm fine, or that I'm not fine, and I'm surely having a heart attack. One of my uncles had a heart attack; what did they say you have to do? Lie down, put my legs in the air? No, that's not right. What is it again? Pinch the bridge of my nose? I don't know, I don't know. Someone help me.

And all the time, my lungs are burning, my windpipe crushing itself. How long have I been standing here? Everything is blurred around the edges. Most of the others have left now: gone to their next class or out towards the pool. My back is against the cold tiled wall and I gasp, and gasp, and gasp for my life.

I, PIGGY-WIG

If you've ever been bullied, you'll know. It's so much more than just the friendly banter and everyday jostle that you're shamed into believing is a rite of passage for all children. It's a cruel and continuous undermining of a person's worth, perpetuated by the attitude that it's just the world's way of toughening you up – doing you a service, you know. A guidance teacher, to whom I'd finally gone for advice after years of harassment, could only offer the wisdom that I was bringing the situation upon myself and should learn to fit in more with my peers, by changing how I dressed, to look more like everyone else. Granted, my spray-painted Doc Martens squeaked against her office floor, as I peered at her sidelong through hair so pink it made flamingos wink, but her suggestion was nonetheless destructive.

The teacher went on to helpfully name particular brands of clothing that might help me earn the respect of classmates who had thus far ripped apart every fibre of my personality as though I was made of Velcro. Sure, a Benetton jumper will do the trick, Miss.

I had taken to embracing alternative culture quite early in my youth, for various reasons, not least of which was that I genuinely loved the philosophy, the music, and the option to just be outside the world that seemed to hate me so much. Looking back though, I guess it was also a decent way of externalising the constant putdowns. If the comments were directed at my clothes and piercings, they weren't actually a comment on me: just on the style I had chosen. An entire school wasn't tormenting me daily because there was something inherently wrong with me; they were offended by the badges on my ripped rucksack and the fishnets I wore over my tights. We just had differing opinions on fashion, and I could handle that.

If hiding in extravagant sight was the only strategy I had to keep facing the bullies, I was going to use it, even if it did mean being called the piggy-wig by a deputy headteacher almost every day, for the ring at the end of my nose, my nose, for the ring at the end of my nose. Probably, he had no idea of the impact of his jibe; probably, he didn't know what I'd been facing for the previous three years in his school; probably, he didn't go home and hear the name over and again in his head. But piggy-wig stuck with me, the way words so stubbornly can. For long enough, it's how I thought of myself, but not as the charming character that the owl and the pussycat's ring-bearer came across.

I was a piggy-wig in all the worst of ways.

WORD ON THE STREET

The car engine revs again. My friend's dad isn't the patient sort. I've known the family long enough to accept his irritability, but I still don't like him much. He's driving us into town though, so it's worth just hurrying up. In fairness, I'm not actually keeping us late; Jackie is never on time, even when she makes the plans and I just go along with them. I've almost had to drag her down the stairs this morning. I don't understand how anyone can take so long to pick an outfit. It's not like there's coordination to cope with: everything we own is black.

BEEP.

The honking horn is sounding angrier by the minute. It makes my stomach jolt. I really don't want another argument to start; the shouting and sniping is so awkward. I never know where to look or what to say. I don't think they even notice they're doing it sometimes.

I try to focus on the other end of the journey instead. I know the centres we'll visit, the windows we'll shop – it's always the same, but it's Saturday and that deserves a celebration. For today and tomorrow, I'm not facing the weekday attacks. I'm free and I'm calm, and I'm allowed to be in the world, just as I am.

BEEP.

We're only waiting for Jackie's mum now. If tardiness is inherited, I know which family line hers followed. I'm climbing into the Volvo's back seat when her mum finally appears at the door with about a thousand bags and a box full of video tapes. I've no idea where they go when they drop us off, and every sensible thought I have tells me not ask. She bumbles towards us, heels clicking on the wet pavement. I've always envied her ability to walk in those five-inch stilettos. Although sometimes it's more up-wrong than upright. She's almost by the open window when he roars from the driver's seat.

'That's never going to fit in the –ing car.'

There we are, it's never far away. She doesn't even falter. He's probably right. I know the car boot is already full of junk and, with four of us aboard, there's not much room on the inside either. It was a fight waiting to happen but, as usual, it didn't have to wait long. I don't doubt there's a rough few minutes ahead, as points are proven and scored. Just keep my head down and wait for it all to settle; that's all I can do now. Stupidly, I don't expect the next words that slip so easily from her mouth, as she drops the box and yanks open the door nearest me. 'If Paula just moves her fat ass, it will.' I shuffle closer to Jackie, trying to make myself as small as I can be. But all I seem to do is get bigger and bigger, filling all the space inside my head.

NIL BY MOUTH

As far as relationships go, mine with food well and truly went during my 14th year. Not overnight, but quickly and progressively, I began to carefully control my diet. I became fussier than a panda on the Atkins diet, counting my calorie intake obsessively, then halving the portion, just to be safe.

I won't lie – guilt gives me hives – but I've always loved to eat. Not that I can cook, nor was I ever a gastronome, but hide half a chocolate bar in a room and I'll seek out that sugar high before you've even started the countdown. Strangely though, before this point, I'd never really considered my weight as an issue. In fact, I'd never considered it at all. In hindsight (where ambiguity goes to die) I probably always erred on the side of curvy, but not so much that the scales ever tipped against me. I was so busy dealing with the state of my insides though, that I genuinely didn't notice the shape of my outside at all.

Until I did. Then it was all I could notice. My dress size suddenly became an inverse measure of my worth. And I could affect it, improve it, so why wouldn't I?

Skipping meals was easy: lunch was first to fall. While before I would quite happily have plumped for the daily special at the nearby chippie, I began to plump for nothing – so that nothing could plump for me. Since my folks annoyingly cared about my wellbeing though, I was rarely allowed to leave for school in the morning without having at least moaned over a bowl of cereal long enough for half its contents to disintegrate. But once or twice a week I could skip out of supper, if I put in the effort. I didn't have the expertise to create a proper diet plan, or the internet to fake it, but I understood a calorie deficit, and was happy enough to use it.

Okay, "happy" isn't quite what I was. Miserable but vindicated is closer to the reality – but sometimes that can feel a lot like joy. For the next few years, I saw my energy levels plummet, my hair start to thin, and my bowels take industrial action. Still it wasn't enough. It could never be enough, I was so convinced I really was a piggy-wig. Thus began my aversion to mirrors, my hatred of photographs, and my fear of eating in public. I didn't need judgement falling upon me while my fat face either said "cheese" or ate it, so I dodged cameras and cafés and put reflective surfaces behind me.

I couldn't quite see the same picture everyone else was painting, and truly I'm not sure I wanted to. I had managed to wrestle back a tiny element of power over my own existence and no one was taking that away from me.

STOP

Stop.

Please just stop. Now.

Maybe I'm not saying it right. Is the sound coming out at all? I can't tell any more. But I try again because there's nothing else I can do.

No. I don't want this.

I didn't even want to be at this stupid party. I only agreed because Jackie begged, and I was the only one who was free on a Saturday night at such short notice. Plus, I negotiated to wear her velvet dress that I've always thought I'd look better in than I actually do right now. It wasn't worth it.

He doesn't seem to care though: this boy pretending he's a man because he's spent a few more years learning nothing at our school. And because he's taller and broader and stronger than I am. He's hurting me because he can, because I can't stop him, but still he's trying to bargain with me. As though he can talk me around and that'll make it alright somehow. But if he's doing this, he's doing it without my permission. I know that, if nothing else.

Stop.

I've seen him in the corridors, I know his name and his friends, but I don't know him, not really. And I don't know how I got myself into this situation. I should have just stayed home. This was stupid. I'm stupid. I should have known better. I should have been more careful. I can never tell anyone about this. Not anyone. I know what they say about girls that end up here, right where I am. I can't take that. I just can't. I push him again, but he doesn't even notice. And I've run out of fight.

No.

Then I stay quiet. I just stay quiet.

CHAPTER 4

ADVENTURES IN THE REAL WORLD

I finally escaped high school in 1997. Suddenly, *The Real World* was no longer just a quirky MTV show, all shiny hair and personalities – and I had to actually start living in it. Gulp.

I was 16 years old with a place in the accounting degree programme of a great university, and I was terrified. I spent the summer in a daze, wondering if this was just a step too big for my podgy little legs, but the pride of having not only survived five years of bullying, but having robbed the bullies of that final year of persecuting me gave me that much-needed extra spring.

Besides, school was the place where young people were forced to be learners, day by mandatory day. I was about to move on to the place where learners opted to attend, where thoughts were free, where minds were comfortably alike but progressively different. This was to be the bright new world I had always dreamt education would be; this was to be my home, these were to be my people. And I'm pretty sure they would have been my people, had I not been a frightened 16-year-old with a broad intellect but a very narrow set of social skills, and had they not been several years older with a point to prove around wisdom. Hanging out with an under-ager, who could have written the book on imposter syndrome, had she not been such a bloody fraud, would do nothing for a fresher's street cred. By the time I was old enough to legally visit my own Student Union bar, we were almost in Third Year and those early cohort bonding sessions had already been drunk dry.

Aside from my age and innate awkwardness, there was one other shortcoming that set me miles apart from the majority of my fellow students: I was from the wrong side of town. Over the coming years, I endured being suddenly avoided and removed from conversations, lost marks for my presentation group because of my sloppy pronunciation, and was told repeatedly that I was only accepted onto the course in order that the school met its "working class quota". It didn't help that none of my family had ever been to university or had any connection with accounting, or that I had been awarded a scholarship to support my studies. Granted, my heart wasn't particularly in the subject; I had essentially opened the prospectus at A and applied for the first subject that didn't require a four-year supply of ants. I was 15 and desperate to find any emergency exit out of school that didn't lead to jail or destitution – what did I know about long-term decision-making? Clearly not much. The Real World, apparently, expects you to take career advice.

If it seems like I'm missing out large swathes of my life as we're trundling through this story, it's probably because I am. Not for any misplaced embarrassment or attempt to spare you the gories, but because anxiety robbed me of so many of the memories that I should, by rights, be relating. There are periods of my past, sometimes important and formative experiences, that I couldn't recount now with a crystal ball and an abacus. They're all fog and frenzy, and no matter how hard I try to engage with those moments, they disintegrate before I can ever see them through.

Anxiety removes you from the world, and from situations and opportunities, without you ever realising it. You're sure that you are there, right at the centre even, but you aren't, not really. Anxiety forces you so deep into your own head that everything outside of those rapidly firing synapses no longer exists, except to remind you how worried you really should be, and then restart the cycle. You move through your own life, never quite touching the sides, never with the space to latch on to those individual pieces that will, in time, be your connection back to them. The tree that stood out on the landscape, the song that filled the room: I didn't have the wherewithal to grip on to those markers, to store them away for the future, so busy was I coping with just being around them. And now, they're gone, lost, just gaps in my tale. They're all just ... BLANK ...

Here, I'll show you ...

LIFE, INTERRUPTED

We've reached the building that the photocopied map seems to suggest will hold the registration session for my course. I turn it around a few times, angle it towards my dad for confirmation, and he nods without really knowing. I can always tell. But I'm so glad he's here, walking me towards my first official day of university. It's only a 25-minute walk from home but, as usual, I managed to make sure we left almost an hour too early, so I can definitely afford another few rotations of the map.

As much as this is my first official day here, it's also the first time I've actually visited the campus, since every other event before this has been optional. And given the option, I would push my start date all the way back to never. Not that I don't want to be here: living and learning, it's the dream. I just don't want to have to actually start, to have to walk through those glass doors and figure it all out. I want a manual to read at home or a pass straight through to familiarity, but instead all I have is a room number and a contact name, and a hug from my dad that says everything else I need to know. He's proud of me – and if he doesn't walk away now, he'll be crying before my next step.

I muster courage and stumble into the stream of people heading for the entrance. I've never seen the inside of a university building before and ...

... BLANK ...

The guy sitting on the bench next to me just pointed out that my elective subject isn't on the schedule. He's the only person I've managed to speak to so far but, in a room so full of strangers, I'm delighted that there's now at least one face I know: William. Maybe I've been worrying for nothing; maybe making friends here will be easy, after all. Easier, at least.

Now though, I'm panicking that my timetable is incomplete, since there's one subject missing altogether. French. Who picks French alongside an accounting degree? Idiots who want to draw attention to themselves at course registration, that's who. I should just raise my hand and let the lecturer know. Actually, do you raise your hand here? Or is that just a school thing? Either way, I can't seem to force myself to move.

I'm pretty sure we're meant to be heading somewhere now; everyone is shuffling around, gathering belongings and strength for the onward journey. My hands and I stay just where we are. I've missed the announcement.

Then I hear my name being called and I catch the eye of the lecturer, whose name is falling out of my short-term memory more quickly than my gaze drops to the carpet-tiled floor. I'll have to go over. I can't just ignore him.

... BLANK ...

I'm nodding as the woman in the Modern Languages office talks me through combinations of classes that might fit my Business School curriculum. She's already scribbled over the only copy I have of this semester's timetable, and I've only just learnt the word "semester" so I don't think I can trust myself to memorise the class list too. I think what she's saying is that I can still take French, as long as I have the ability to be in two different rooms in the furthest apart departments at the same time each week. What I'm quickly learning about higher education is that they'll lay out all the facts for you, but it's up to you to make your own truth.

William has kindly traipsed along with me, and sits in the hallway. At least, I think that's him.

... BLANK ...

The bus looks packed, as I join the queue to board. The windows are steamy, but I can see the figures standing by the doors, crammed together, trying not to look at those they're inadvertently touching. I'm not sure how long I've been waiting at the stop. Longer than most; I'm not great with public transport. There are far too many opportunities for faux pas, and I'm tired of mix-ups today – French or otherwise. The driver cranes his neck to look at me, confused as to whether or not I want on. I start to walk home. The streets are busy so I move quickly, weaving in and out, hoping not to be noticed.

... BLANK ...

PAINS, STRAINS, AND AUTO-BUSES

Then I graduated.

Fine, there are one or two details in the four intervening years that stuck, but not many more than that. Mostly, they're people. William, who, even after that patchy first day, remained my closest friend throughout our university stretch, and without, I'm sure, knowing it, saved my anxious skin many times. The fellow student who told me, week on week, that I was only there to make up the numbers. The senior lecturer who encouraged me whenever I lagged.

Maybe that's enough. Perhaps I don't need to remember the minutiae: the double taxation lectures and 12-hour library sessions. It might indeed be better for my sensitive soul not to be able to hark back to every snub and shortcoming. And if my anxiety had stopped there, I guess I wouldn't be quite so irritated by its actions. But, of course, it didn't. Anxiety continued, over the subsequent 10 years, to steal more and more from my memory bank, until it might as well have worn a balaclava. As I continued to fall to its seemingly superior will, I lost parts of the story that should have been sacrosanct: holidays and Saturday mornings, family moments that now, I only know anecdotally. Constantly in the eye of my own mental storm, separated from everyone and everything by the squall of fear and regret, I struggled to find my footing on what was becoming increasingly unsettled terrain. You see, since the age of four and a half, when my first teacher told my mum I was headed for university, my path had always been completely in view. Whatever was happening on either side, as long as I kept within its borders, I could plough on regardless, following its length to where I was so sure I belonged. But then it stopped; not with a gate to a whole new experience, but with an end so dead it deserved a funeral.

If my studies taught me anything, it's that I'm not an accountant. In a job interview, I was asked to describe the most interesting thing

I'd found in that morning's financial presses. I spent around 12 minutes talking about the incredible use of language that had almost convinced me to care about the stock market. I never quite satisfied the panel that I was right for that job – or any other. The corporate world wasn't built for self-consciousness and reserve, and I wasn't built of much else.

Suddenly, I was a 20-year-old graduate with expectation's weight on already shaking shoulders. So, of course, the only thing to do was become a bus driver! And I'm pretty sure I would have been a good one too, if it wasn't for having to pick up passengers. The training was a joy; cruising around in a single-decker, wearing borrowed boots three sizes too big because my own size fours just wouldn't influence the pedals. I could do this; in fact, my reverse parking was so accurate I considered travelling everywhere tail-first. After a week or two though, the test neared, and the reality of the job broke through the distraction of an empty bus and professional road-trip. Before long, people would be expecting to join me on my moving haven; people I didn't know and wasn't sure I could face. The truth hit me finally on an afternoon training run, when a woman mistakenly tried to hail our learner coach and, instead of slowing to explain, I accelerated off with all the force of my second-hand shoes, and shook with nerves the whole way back to the depot. The conversation with my supervisor was brief and I headed home from another road block with just one more sign that I wasn't quite right for the world.

A year of unemployment will do a lot for a person, mainly using verbs like "damage" and "destroy". It's kind that way. To me, unemployment gave time and space not only to ruminate on just how awful I was at being an adult, but to grow more into that mindset and really adopt the part. Whether I was over or under qualified didn't really matter; I was never quite qualified by anyone's standards, and that kind of water doesn't slide off even the slipperiest of duck's backs.

Eventually, I landed a 10-week contract in the Inland Revenue's mail room, even after falling over the same chair on the way into and out of the interview. It was my first real job, and I was 21, with no idea how to fit in to a workplace. No combination of round and square holes could accommodate this peg. Luckily, the bustle of a busy post room is exactly the kind of environment in which a nervous new-start can hide, until such time as she knows what she's doing. And, in spite of the monotony of the work and the rowdy atmosphere, I settled in pretty quickly, and made friends I hope never to lose; friends who didn't seem to notice my twitchy face, or mind my idiosyncrasies.

Of course, managing growing anxiety while pretending you're just another "normal" person requires some trickery and mental toughness. Sadly, I had neither in my armoury, so quickly began to dissolve into a puddle of crazy. Becoming more superstitious by the day, I was spending my tea breaks touching wood so that I wouldn't break a mirror, and then my lunch, removing the splinters. I was already heavily medicated and quickly fell into drug dependency to survive each working day. Before a seven o'clock start, I would be at least six painkillers down, with a stash in my locker to see me through the shift – on top of the anxiety pills I'd already tipped back. And since eating in public had long been an issue, mostly I would just starve my way through the working week, explaining away my absence at meal-times with fad diet excuses and mumblings.

As the temporary contract turned permanent, I became less and less stable, and my mental health crept ever closer to the edge.

Throughout it all though, my productivity never waned, since doing a good job was something I could actually control. So before long I was promoted, moved departments and – oh, God no – expected to make phone calls, have meetings, and talk to strangers. Every. Single. Day. I coped, for a little while, washing stress down with tension; abusing annual leave and dodging difficult tasks.

Then, all at once, I broke.

BREAK-TIME

I'm shaking. I can't stop. It's been three days.

I've woken up in my parents' bed again. Although I'm not sure I was ever asleep.

I can't be on my own.

It's not fair; I know it isn't. Mum taking time off work. Dad sleeping downstairs. Like I'm a child.

But I can't be on my own.

Mum holds my hand. She talks to me. I know she's worried.

There's nothing wrong with me. The doctor has been. I'm not sick.

I don't think I'll survive. I can't picture tomorrow. I don't even want to.

I can handle the shaking. Even the crying. Just not the emptiness.

I can feel everything. And nothing at all. It rushes at me, overwhelming. Every thought, altogether. Flushing me through. Leaving me. Alone. All at once.

What if it ends right here? In a sweat-sodden bed.

What if it never ends?

I can't be on my own.

A FRAGILE PEACE

The breakdown lasted five days.

During that time, I couldn't go to the toilet without a member of my family standing outside the half-open door, talking to me continuously. In the afternoons, I lay, sat, knelt, rocked on the sofa, unable to be still for more than a beat. At night, I curled up in my mum's arms and sobbed until exhaustion relieved me. I'd been given more medication from the doctor to calm the panic but was too scared to take it. It's near impossible to describe despair at that level and, trust me, they've sent many a poet to try. Hopelessness comes close but doesn't convey the fractured thoughts, the loss of connection, the simple agony of being.

On the sixth day, I just woke up. Nothing had changed, except that everything was different. I tiptoed downstairs at 4.30am and drank tea by myself at the open window; alone for the first time in almost a week. I spent the rest of the morning tidying and organising; full of a drive that I didn't recognise. By the weekend, my energy levels had evened out, but I felt that the worst was over. For now.

The following Monday I returned to work, opting to give up the promotion and revert back to the stability of my previous role. I had survived, but with cracks. I now knew just how fragile my grip on sanity actually was, and how easily I could let go. I was so scared to go back there that every slight slip took on new and terrifying meaning. I became even more careful with myself; finding excuses to dodge anything that might cause another crash.

Coping techniques that were once merely filigree were now the very pillars of my days. I wasted hours travelling to new places the night before I was due there, just to check out where the meeting rooms, exits, toilets were, so as to avoid having to ask for directions or look lost. I began to spend more time than ever alone; the only place I knew I couldn't embarrass myself. Social situations that I might once have found the courage to attend out of friendship or duty were wiped from my calendar completely, until eventually I stopped being invited. As you can imagine, I'd never exactly been the life and soul anyway, and I certainly wasn't the spirit, since I've never drunk more than the total of tea. As a teenager, when pubs and clubs became our new playground, the fun for me was in spending time in crowds, unidentifiable as an individual among the throng. But the thought of losing control, of embarrassing myself without even knowing it, was intolerable so booze was not on my menu. I quickly became the self-designated sober friend, then driver; making sure that everyone – including my reputation – made it home safely. I've since tried gin once, at the age of 35, and stand by my original opinion.

Even at the most difficult of times, I continued to work as hard and, seemingly, as well as possible, since I couldn't bear for anyone to think I wasn't able to function as a responsible adult. Day-to-day, I managed, and I reckon I did a pretty good job of convincing people that my nerves were within normal levels, not spiking off the charts (as they so often were).

After a few years, I moved from my post-room job into support work, and I found real joy in helping others to find a freedom that was ever more escaping me. I had volunteered in a similar role throughout university, becoming comfortable as a sighted guide for visually impaired people, and the transition to working with deafblind people as a guide / communicator was more natural than I expected. Surprisingly, speaking up on someone else's behalf wasn't a fraction as tough as voicing my own opinions and, in spite of the stressful, and often incredibly challenging nature of the work, it seemed to fit well with my nature. While I couldn't shop on my own, or face appointments by myself, I was able to guide another person around supermarkets and doctors' surgeries, ensuring that their lives were as full as mine was empty. The intensity of the tasks gave me focus, outside of myself, at least for a short while each day. And then there was Gerry; the charity's Information Officer, who I was somehow both comfortable and exhilarated around in almost equal quantities.

Beyond that though, I was crumbling, without any sign of the glue needed to put me back together. And, trust me, I had looked: under every medical intervention and even the least reputable treatments. The latest response from my local mental health services insisted that there was nothing more that could be done to help me, and, you know what, I believed them.

Across all those years of suffering, I had tried everything to quell the anxiety that was so sure to drown me. But while I was taking all the pills that science could provide, and attending therapy sessions that were more quack than a flock of ducks, I was gradually removing myself from the one thing in which I would finally find respite: the rest of the world.

THINGS I TRIED TO CURE MY ANXIETY

- **Medication:** All the medication, both prescribed and over the counter, at times without heed of maximum dosage or contraindications. I've been a zombie, a crier, a breathless recluse, and I know one thing: pills can really help, as long as you follow direction, and support your recovery with chat and self care. 10 years of just topping up the tablets and hoping the next four would save my sanity, only served to mire me in addiction and send the local pharmacist on a cruise.
- **Homeopathy:** I'm pretty sure the water has better memory of its effect on me than I do.
- **Hypnotherapy:** Wrapped in a warm blanket and with a perfectly soothing voice guiding me into what should at least have been a decent nap, the hypnotherapy process should have been a delight. But, for my racing, rushing mind, letting go of its grip on reality in the presence of just one stranger was a release too far. I spent the entire session worrying that the therapist would be offended that I was still awake.
- **Counselling:** There aren't many health conditions that you can have any impact on just by talking about them, but anxiety is definitely one of them. The kicker is that you're so anxious about seeming normal, you can't bring yourself to admit the problem. Shame and embarrassment stopped me from properly engaging with talking therapies, even though I tried, over and again. But at least I got that shoplifted lollipop off my chest!

- **Acupuncture:** Sticking pins in problems seemed like as good a way forward as any and, while I found real enjoyment in each tiny individual puncturing, it probably says more about my inclinations than the treatment.
- **Alternative therapies:** Candles in my ears, tinctures in my tea, crystals every which way. Some helped, calming my mind for hours, even days; some were oil straight from the snake. I'll admit though, some of the therapies I invited into my system weren't so much alternative as downright avant-garde. I was so desperate to be cured that if you'd told me you had magic beans, I'd have swapped you my prized cow before you could say "lactose intolerant".
- **Diet:** I think it's fair to say that food and I are not natural bedfellows. For one thing, I can't abide crumbs in the sheets. But I've always been able to make space for sugar and caffeine, and all those things that stimulate my already wired brain. I've changed my eating so many times it's become a habit; every food group finding its way onto or off my shopping list at one point or another. It turns out though that a stable eating pattern is the only recipe that really feeds my mental health – with a little of what I fancy on the side, of course.
- **Research:** I'll tell you what, I love a bit of research. Give me a topic and I'll bring you back a history as potted as your aspidistra. Trying to absorb every ounce of science and supposition about what might or might not be working in my whirling brain, however, was not always the healthiest way to calm it. I'd probably have been better with an adrenaline shot.
- **Avoidance:** If it scares you, stop it. If it worries you, shun it. Do nothing, try nothing, fail nothing. Avoid, avoid, avoid. On the leader-board of strategies, this one ranked just above exorcism but somehow became my first choice. Eventually, there was nothing much left to cut out.

- **Boxing it all up:** Somewhere around my early twenties, I began to write down my most obnoxious worries, whenever anxiety had me pinned to the wall, and put them in a pretty box. I'm not sure where the idea came from, or even if the prettiness of the box actually mattered, but, at times, it helped; not to take the anxiety away, but to give me a kind of priority system so I'd know what I should be worried about and when. It looked a little like this ...

THE BOX OF WORRIES

There have been three natural disasters in the last month.

So many people have died and I can't do anything about it.

What if it never stops?

What can I do?

I can't stop thinking about it.

I said something stupid at work today.

Three people heard me. They didn't say anything, but I know they heard.

I wish I hadn't opened my mouth.

It's better when I just don't talk.

Maybe I should apologise.

Tomorrow. I'll try to apologise tomorrow.

Or send a card.

Just to let them know I haven't forgotten.

I can't get out of going to this wedding.

It's in a fortnight and I'm already not sleeping. I don't know if I can cope with it.

I have all these crazy thoughts about what will go wrong.

I know they're ridiculous. I know I'm being ridiculous.

But everyone will be chatting and dancing. I don't know how to do that.

I won't cope.

My left arm has been tingling all night.

I think I'm going to die.

CHAPTER 5

ADVENTURES IN (AND OUT) OF LOVE

There's nowt, so they say, as queer as folk. And I would know, given that I rank high among the queerest. The wonderful strangeness of the human race though is, by definition, what makes us special. Our consciousness allows for expression beyond that of basic functionality and since we, for the most part, no longer spend our waking hours stalking a lunch that doesn't even bring its own dressing, our attention and energies are driven in more creative directions. Of course, with extra capacity comes extra room for self-reflection – and I, for one, hate mirrors. Perhaps anxiety wouldn't have found me had I opted to evolve with the other hominid species instead. I'm pretty sure Neanderthals didn't fret over the relative size of their tools day-to-day. They also skipped out on the social skills seminar so, in that respect at least, I would fit right in.

Being around people, joining in and finding a place to belong, is such a basic instinct that it seems ridiculous to even bring it up in adult conversation, never mind dedicate an entire chapter to the subject. And while I'd truly love to subvert expectations here by telling you that the rest of these pages describe the plain sailing that has been my love life, sails have unfortunately never been quite so elaborate. Navigating the labyrinth that is human interactions is, I don't doubt, a tricky trek for everyone. Lump anxiety onto the scene though and you might as well just set the maze alight. Too quiet, too chatty, too honest, too clingy, too much, too little: who put all these limits on what is socially acceptable, and why wasn't I given the rulebook? Every time I met a new person throughout life, I was faced not only with trying to remember those rules, but also with the impression that everyone else had memorised them already. I was starting out three steps behind without the puff to ever catch up. Friends that I made through childhood were mostly by dint of our whereabouts: wherever they were, I was (and I wasn't much hassle to have around). Throw me a book and your jacket and I'll basically wait out whatever you're doing. You won't find a more loyal companion, and you don't even need to tie me to a lamppost. But making new friends – in spite of my skill with modelling clay – has always been a test of my character; one in which my grade never really improved.

After the assault that marked the end of my adolescence, you could say that I wasn't quite sure how to move forwards. You could say it, and you would be right. It changed things for me, even though I neither disclosed, nor actually dealt with it at the time, for all the reasons that you would expect. I'd never been in any way comfortable around people and now, it seemed, that uneasiness was vindicated, in ways I hadn't considered. I was always so busy being concerned about their opinions of me, that I hadn't even considered the danger they might pose. Trusting their intentions became increasingly difficult and, if you weren't already on my safe list, there was no way I'd be adding your name. In that way, I fell into my first romance, feet first, and with no sight of what I was in for.

She was a friend, already vetted by my messed-up defence system, and she made me feel safe – well, safer. Off we trotted in wide-eyed hope, and, yes, the thrill of young love, at a time when the world was already growing too big for my narrowed eyes. It was never a healthy situation, neither of us was really there for the right reasons, and the faith we had in the friendship wasn't justified. Across a few years, that faith was consistently broken, then patched back together in what was, shall we say, a tumultuous affair. And I shall say it: this relationship rivalled botox in toxicity, if not in sensation. The end came with whimpering defeat and we walked away, no longer friends, but neither enemies.

If I'm painting a picture of bohemian freedoms here, please excuse my misplaced brushwork: I'm no Picasso. For the most part, I was simply following the path of least resistance, downhill all the way. Only after a few healthier, more stable relationships did I start to recognise that people didn't just happen to me, that I could happen to them too. As in every part of my past though, anxiety thread itself like a neon ribbon through each connection I made; ruining the weakest, testing even the strongest. It's hard to convince someone you are worth living with, when you're not wholly sure you want to live with yourself.

Without trying, I pushed people away or held them too close – sometimes both, mere moments apart. I was always there to listen, to support, to bolster and encourage, but at times, all folk want is to head down the pub, and I just couldn't be there for that. So I missed them and, before long, they realised they weren't really missing me. Eventually, there were a few stalwart friends who saw me for what I was, and expected nothing more. Even for them though, I know it wasn't easy to understand some of my less sensible actions ...

THINGS ANXIETY MADE ME DO

- Carry a wooden clothes peg around in my pocket for almost three years, in case the need arose to touch wood in a purely man-made setting. Her name was Peggy. Superstition is a bitch; Peggy wasn't.
- Develop astonishing bladder control. When you can't pee in public toilets because the acoustics make you sound like the

Victoria Falls, full days at school or work, or even a particularly protracted conversation, require true dedication to the cause. The cause, of course, being not continuously wetting yourself. My pelvic floor's so stiff, it could be screeded.

- Climb 22 flights of stairs because, in a lift, even two's a crowd. Maximum capacity means nothing when you're hauling a tonne of terror.
- Wear multiple pairs of pants with every outfit, just in case. It's an anxiety thing.
- Chew gum with every cup of tea for so many years – because I was so concerned that my breath might smell otherwise – now it's the only way I can have a hot beverage.
- Pretend to have a bad back for a full year of primary school, in order to avoid a once-a-fortnight gym class. The performance involved limps, pained expressions and forgeries. The reviews – from both parents and teacher – were mixed.
- Eat half an uncooked pie because three-day food poisoning is less awkward than telling someone they can't cook.
- Shave my legs with scissors, as there were no female assistants on shift at the chemist and I wasn't buying razors from a dude.
- Spend at least an hour before any five-minute phone call to a shop, making flowcharts of every potential direction in which the conversation might go, only to miss the opening times, and be forced to repeat the process the next day.
- Stand in a dark cupboard for a carefully calculated space of time instead of admitting to trying to find the toilet and picking the wrong door.
- Lose bodily functions through excessive stress and starving myself. (I didn't say they were all funny.)
- Pay £200 in charges rather than facing the call to the bank to pay the original bill.

- Walk a 12-mile round trip in the snow because the bus fares weren't immediately obvious, and like hell was I asking the driver for clarification.
- Almost ruin the first date with my now-husband by being too scared to eat in his company ...

A POCKETFUL OF CRUMBS

I order dry toast and tea. Dry toast. For lunch. In a café.

Gerry doesn't miss a beat, nor give any indication that there's anything odd about my meal of choice, or the fact that I've steered us towards the table in the darkest corner of the shop, almost inside the disabled toilet.

He asks for some coffee configuration that I've never heard of, and a normal person's lunch dish – sandwiches, with actual fillings and the like. He doesn't seem to care that the guy with the notepad has checked twice that all I want is toast.

That's the moment I know.

It's not only the toast thing though. He somehow seems to get it. Or maybe anxiety just isn't on his watch-list at all. We've known each other a while now, chatted in the office whenever I've passed by, so he must have picked up on how nervous I am all the livelong day. Still though, he asked me to catch up outside work, has spent almost an hour in my company on a Saturday morning, and hasn't once asked why I blink so bloody much. I love him already.

'Did you see the sunset last night?'

I realise I've been staring, as his voice breaks my concentration. 'Where?'

Bloody hell, Paula, in the sky. Sort yourself out. Gerry laughs as I try and fail not to look embarrassed. His eyes are bluer than I've ever noticed. Maybe it's the light in the café; maybe it's the light from the games console he brought to show me his holiday photos. Either way, I'm glad they're here, angled in my direction. He's piecing together the deconstructed coffee that's been plonked before him by a disinterested waitress, and I use the distraction to start breaking my pale toast into pieces as small as would seem reasonable.

Of course, Gerry doesn't know that I can't eat in public. Why would he? It's not exactly the kind of thing you assume about folk. I had really hoped we might just head out for a quiet walk, or sit in the car for a bit, you know, like people who meet on the internet and don't want their spouses to find out. But no, this one is all legitimate and sincere – and I have to do everything in my power to pretend that I'm absolutely cool with the diners at the next bench sometimes looking this way, or the tea I've just dripped down my chin or ... I'm a mess, I'm a mess, oh God, I'm a mess.

As casually as I can manage, I drop a piece of crust to the floor beneath my chair, then instantly regret it since someone will have to pick up after me, as usual. I don't think he spotted it though. The next piece goes in my handbag, as I rummage inside for a tissue. The tissue takes two bits back from where it came.

Gerry talks comfortably, and makes me laugh before I've had a chance to vet the noise I might make. I'm never relaxed but, right now, I'm not completely ill at ease either. He never seems bothered by the presence of strangers; I don't even think he's aware of them, of their opinions or judgement. Whereas I'm never unaware of them.

He eats noisily, enjoying every bite, while I shrink further into my chair, continuing to shred my lunch and dispose of the crumbs. He's mannerly and attentive, but without a hint of obligation. He's not trying to be, or not be, anything. He just is. And it's beautiful to watch.

I make my excuses to nip to the toilet, just to check that I haven't, by some means or other, managed to end up with food on my face, and try to act as though I don't care that I've no idea where I'm going. It's not exactly a vast expanse to traverse; it's a café in the west end.

I'm pretty sure I won't need a Sherpa. But by the time I've reached the ladies', I've already tripped over two chair legs and got in the way of a man carrying a heap of plates. If only I wasn't so clumsy, life would be a damn sight easier – and a whole lot less hazardous for everyone involved. Now, I must beat myself up for at least three minutes because heaven forbid I get through a day without ritual self-loathing.

I steel myself for the return journey, hopeful that Gerry didn't witness the first lap. He just waves across the room though, and once again, I'm struck by how well he fits the world – or how little he cares that he doesn't. By one method or another, we've finished our food, and I'm relieved to be heading for the door, but a part of me really doesn't want a way out.

It's April and the leafy streets still rustle with a cool spring breeze. Gerry takes my hands in his as we walk, and breathes warmly onto my freezing fingers for far too short a moment. We're almost back at the car but he stops.

'Do you mind if we just nip into Maplin for a minute?' Somehow, I don't mind one little bit.

ME, HIM AND US

I told Gerry I loved him on our second date. The words just fell out. Less than a year later he proposed. I guess he felt the same. I think he still does.

Our early courtship was hilarious, as his composure crashed into my neuroses, and we bumbled around the resulting muddle. While that could so easily have been off-putting for anyone with a hint of self-preservation, Gerry's reaction was never to pull away or try to drag me into his reality. He stood firm, by my side, frustrated by my anxiety, but never by me.

As a child, my family grew into the role of supporting me, adapting to each new symptom and struggle as it arose. Somehow, here was this latest arrival in my life, who, within days, seemed to understand how it was done. We never even really had the conversation:

'I have social anxiety. I don't like leaving the house. People scare me. I take a lot of medication. We can't go to parties. I'll probably never meet your friends. I thought I'd die alone.' 'Okay ...'

It just didn't need to be said, thankfully. Anxiety was simply an extra facet of our relationship – like the first kiss, or the kids talk; something we would work out as things developed. Each new situation brought a different challenge, but we'd adapt. It was a process, and the learning curve was more of a hairpin, but at last I'd found something exciting and scary from which I knew I could never shy away.

For the first time, I was learning to find the humour in my madness. Not in the moment, of course, but later. Once I'd written my apologies, and cried for a few hours, we would talk it all through and he'd smile and, suddenly, so would I. It helped to know that whatever horror the world threw at me, and however poorly I coped, I could always rely on Gerry to help me turn to face the funny side. He became my blanket – never wrapped too tightly, never stifling, just cuddled around my shoulders for whenever I might need its warmth. It helped that he's big enough for me to hide behind too. While he settled without fuss around my modus operandi though, I couldn't quite cope with the knowledge that every day of us was surely affecting him. I can't imagine how hard it is to love someone who is so swamped in her own head that she's giving herself trench foot. I never meant to be difficult; I've tried so hard every day of my life to make things better for others, but I know that I can't have been fun to be around for large periods of time. When you are so deeply fearful of what tomorrow might bring that you can't possible engage with today, you miss all those opportunities for joy and, worse, you make others miss them too.

Mostly, I still ducked out of social gatherings, and Gerry would turn up with an excuse in lieu of a girlfriend. When the planets aligned though, and I managed to make it to a get-together, Gerry would do the together bit while I would focus on just getting in, getting by and getting straight back out. All the while, he couldn't leave my side, in case a person – strange or stranger – decided that I was someone worth talking to in his absence. Even just a trip to the bathroom was a staged affair, with a trusted cast of supporting characters and a stable backdrop against which I could lean.

As a couple though, we were solid and, one by one, the milestones crept up. We bought a flat and had the shortest engagement possible, since I couldn't handle the prolonged stress of a big build-up. Gerry changed jobs and I quit mine, leaping into self-employment with a terrified enthusiasm. After work, I would gabble irritably about all those things I'd managed to screw up that day, while Gerry patiently talked me back from the edge. He'd carefully remind me it was more than likely no one else had noticed that I couldn't work out how to use the new hand-drier, so damped down my hair with the excess water instead, and left looking like a Robert Palmer backing dancer.

Throughout it all, he saw the good in me. He knew my potential, although I'd hidden it so well I couldn't quite remember where I'd put it. While he so badly wanted me to be able to transfer the person I was with him outside – to the world at large – not once did he push me to change.

What he did instead was give me a reason to want to.

BELLS AND WHISTLE-STOPS

'Are you sure?'

Dad and I are standing at the foot of the church stairs, my arm looped through his. I straighten his teal tie, and smile. He looks more nervous than I am; although I'm almost certain he hasn't taken any medication this morning, while I'm rattling with the stuff. He shuffles his feet a little on the tiled floor, and we laugh at his ridiculous shoes, sourced online, at the last minute, to match his new suit. He looks like a cowboy from the ankles down. But, boy, does he look proud from the neck up.

'Of course.'

I've never been more sure of anything. He knows that.

'I wouldn't be much of a father if I didn't check though.'

I'm sure he went through this same routine with my sister, on her wedding day a few years ago. Luckily this time, he doesn't have a speech to worry about; he barely managed three words of the one he'd prepared for Donna and Paul's reception, before bursting into tears and sitting back down. The photographer didn't have time to even capture the moment.

We've cut out the speeches entirely from our celebration, along with the first dance and top table: anything that could set us apart from the rest of the congregated party. Fine, I'm the one in the ivory dress but, all in all, I think we've done a decent job of keeping things as low key as a wedding allows. I've felt extremely guilty at times during the short planning of our big day that I'm robbing Gerry of so many elements of what should be his special moment too. He should be able to address our guests in his own words, if he so desires. He should have the choice to take to the floor with his new bride, if that's what takes his fancy. He doesn't have the option. It just wouldn't be possible for me to cope with such attention, even in so positive a way.

Of course, he has made it easy; not worrying about what was lost of the wedding, as long as the marriage is built on healthy grounds. And now, somehow, he's waiting at the other end of the church to agree to be hitched to this cracked wagon for the rest of time.

'Oh yes, Dad, I'm sure.'

The opening bars of Pachelbel's Canon flood my ears, as we climb the first step towards the congregation – and the future. I know that when we round the corner at the head of the stairs, I'll be met by the sight of the people we love; all willing me on, full of smiles and hope. I'm instantly terrified, but strangely my pace doesn't falter. This is right where I should be and, for once, anxiety won't convince me to run in the opposite direction.

The walk down the aisle is a blur. There are faces all around that I know I recognise, but I just can't pull back from memory. Aunts and nephews, friends and siblings; everyone that matters. They're polished and shiny, and I want to stop and tell them all just how much each curl and cufflink means to me. But Dad's even stride urges me ever forwards. I'm wearing heels and carrying a wire basket of flower petals but everything else is simple, recognisable me.

Then there's Gerry. In kilted splendour but with nerves showing, like I've never seen, around those familiar eyes. I join him at the altar's edge. We touch hands and at once I'm calmed; back home, in safety, where I belong. As long as we're married by the end of this afternoon, nothing else really matters. I don't think I've ever felt this depth of focus; when just one thing in my mind cuts through all the other crap.

The ceremony is whirling past and I can't quite keep hold of it. We forget to kneel, we cry, we sing with voices garbled by emotion, and we vow to never let go of one another.

And we're married. There's a ring on my finger and, if someone suggested I put bells on my toes, I'd probably be alright with it. In spite of it all – every stupid thing I say, every spiral I fall into – someone incredible, astute, charming, and kind has chosen to be part of my mixed-up world.

It's not too far for even our least mobile guests to wander over the road to the local bowling club for a buffet and a beer. Having a reception was a major compromise, since I originally wanted to send everyone home straight after the ceremony. Maybe post them a piece of my brother-in-law's incredible cake later in the week. Of course, neither set of parents was having that – 'we'd never live it down' – so a party was agreed. Just a party though; good music, cheap rounds, and a decent dance-floor. No pomp, no palaver and, above all else, no pressure. So even when the top tier falls on the floor, and the head of the cake-topper's groom rolls between our feet, even when a guest drips sauce all down the front of my wedding dress, even when a cousin collapses with exhaustion during The Slosh, nothing is ruined because nothing was ever really expected.

I'd never cared about being married in my life. I didn't plan it or hope for it, the way some always do. I'd never really thought it would happen; not to me. But now that it has, I can't imagine caring about anything more.

Gerry and I sit on the floor of our flat's hall, as I pull kirby grips from my hair and wince at the scalp-ache. We're surrounded by unopened cards and presents, on our little island of carpet, and I'm already babbling on about making lists and writing thank-you notes. 'Tomorrow,' Gerry says. And I'm right there with him.

CHAPTER 6

ADVENTURES IN SHAME

If I had bumped into my old self in the street a few years back, like in some ill-advised time-travel TV drama, I don't think I would have recognised the person I had become. Although the fact that a wormhole would probably have opened up in space-time to drag one of us screaming all the way to non-existence would probably have given me a heads up.

To describe myself at the depths of my mental ill health, I'd be forced to use a fair few words that aren't really acceptable in polite company. Not that I'm making any assumptions about your own sensibilities. There's no pressure around these parts; this is a safe space for bad language. I was born in Glasgow, where swearing is just another form of punctuation. But I'll refrain from elaborating, only because I'm not sure my self-esteem could take it. In short, I wasn't the person that my moral compass expected to find at the end of its travels.

I didn't really mean to be any of those terrible things. Like everyone else, I was just trying to make it through each day as best I could and, if that meant compromising my principles here or there to survive the onslaught, then I was willing to make the allowance. In the end, I was compromising both here *and* there. Often, I couldn't find a middle ground that wasn't in a different county from my original viewpoint.

Not to excuse myself in any way but I'd really rather you didn't think I'm a monster by the end of this chapter. I'm not proud of the way I handled my anxiety – or frequently mishandled it – but I never felt that there was another option. You aren't given a handbook with your diagnosis. There's no easy-to-use index of how to cope in situations that are so alien to how an anxious mind works that they might as well have spaceships. I promise I'm not trying to dilute my own responsibility here; this woman takes her blame neat. At times though, thinking straight when everything around seemed so hellishly bumpy just wasn't possible. Thus, I became a whole heap of different versions of Paula – one of them apparently being the type to use "thus" as a sentence opener. None of them, however, would earn me a gold star on the personality chart.

PAULA, THE AWFUL FRIEND

Once upon a time, I was invited to a friend's housewarming party. I know, crazy! Who wants to heat their gorgeous new pad with the coldest fish in the barrel? But all good stories start with an innocent mistake, right? Look at *Home Alone*. I prepared in exactly the way I always had for such a social occasion: three weeks of anxious anticipation, two recces of the venue to check exits and parking facilities, and at least one major meltdown over potential topics of conversation. I'd even bought a vintage teapot as a gift, since my mate and I had first bonded over our capacity for Tetley. I was all set.

I made it to their street, even driving past the house once or twice, now aglow with all the trappings of a night in full fever. I had promised I would be there; God, I was there, only yards from the front door. But I couldn't force myself to pick up that bloody teapot and brave those few steps towards the celebration. The only big bash I attended that night was one of my very own making, as I beat myself up over and over. Since I was too embarrassed to tell my family I had failed another basic adult assignment, I drove around for five hours, allowing the monotony of the motorway to lull my sorry soul. It also gave me enough time to think up an excuse for not turning up, which everyone would accept but no one would believe.

My friend and his wife never did see that teapot.

PAULA, THE DISAPPOINTMENT

I've disappointed a fair few people in my life. I've probably disappointed a few fair people too, in truth: people who believed in me, who relied on my support, who saw my potential, then watched it squandered. And I'm in there too, disappointed along with the rest of them about what I did or didn't do with the chances I had.

Please don't think there's an ounce of self-pity here though: the only wallowing I do these days is in strawberry bubble bath. While I'm well aware that my mental health condition put me at a disadvantage, I'm not here to separate myself out from actions that, let's face it, I took repeatedly, and then took some more. They're part of what I was, of how I survived and, ultimately, of how I recovered.

There's one disappointment though that still stings as sharply as the day it hit. The day that I missed the funeral of one of the most incredible, caring, astute people in my world, because I couldn't bring myself to face what I knew would be such a well-attended affair. An uncle who had given me so much of his time and his energy when I was growing up. An uncle who became the grandfather I'd never had, in all but name.

It wasn't my first funeral. God knows, if being part of a Catholic family gets you anything, it's an early education in cemetery etiquette. I can't even look at a steak pie these days without feeling like a good cry. But that day, I was weaker than I'd been in a long time; feeling the full might of anxiety weighing upon me. So, while the rest of my family said goodbye, I stayed outside, alone in the car, until the wake – and the chance – was over.

Paula, the ham

For someone who avoided the limelight so much she almost developed rickets, anxiety often put me centre stage in my own dramatic productions. Panic attacks in primary, crying fits so regular you could set your body clock by them, stress nose-bleeds and vomiting bouts and twitch-fests; I was the type of girl that the ancient Greeks would have diagnosed with wandering womb.

Clearly, I wasn't craving the publicity; in fact, my appetite for attention never crept above satiated, thank you very much. As it happens though, being so scared of people looking at you that you actually fall over yourself to dodge their line of vision, often draws more eyes than a portraiture class. I made a scene out of even the stillest landscape; panicking when someone offered me a chip in public, finding a ridiculous reason to leave, rushing off abruptly then apologising for the whole sorry fiasco about an hour later, rather than just eating the damn thing and moving on with my life.

I like chips.

PAULA, THE ADDICT

I'm not sure if I have an addictive personality or if I just really, really like stuff. I mean, really like it, to the point that I don't feel that I need anything else in my life. Stuff has consisted of everything over the years, from a song on repeat for four hours a night, to particular brands of sauce in which everything had to be drowned. I even had a brief obsession with curtain hooks, but doesn't everybody at some point or other?

If I had the wherewithal to delve more deeply into the causes of such behaviours, I guess I'd find that control and attachment were in play, but I've had to draw the self-reflection line somewhere and, I'm afraid, for the moment, my addiction issues fell on the wrong side.

Anyway, for the most part, buying 16 bottles of Irn Bru for an average day trip to the seaside wasn't too much of a hassle, although the walk back to the car with the empties was always a noisy affair.

But then, of course, came the pills ...

PAULA, THE THIEF

My key turns in the lock and I push open the front door of my parents' house. They're not home, but that's the point. I drove Mum to work earlier this afternoon and I waited until Dad's afternoon shift to pop over, so I know I won't be disturbed. Gerry and I only live a few streets away, neither of us wanting to move too far from our families, but the lack of distance has become dangerously convenient for my new habit.

The neighbour nods to me as I turn away from the hall to close the door. I hope she doesn't mention to my folks that I was here, although I visit every day anyway, so she probably thinks less of the interaction than my guilt is forcing me to.

I guess I'm a little jumpy, more jumpy than usual, and there's only one thing that will help. I don't even glance into the living room, where we would normally gather to catch up after a busy day, or nip to the bathroom, (even though I've been out since this morning, and could really do with using the facilities). There's nothing else on my mind though, except the kitchen cupboard that I raid so often nowadays.

The handle is in my palm before I remember shuffling towards it; its familiar plastic smoothness already beginning to calm me. I know how the door squeaks and how to stop it, for times when I'm forced to sneak around when someone else is in the house. I know that the napkins on the top shelf sometimes fall out of their bag, scattering haphazardly across the floor. And I know what's kept inside the box at the front right: the codeine-based painkillers prescribed for Mum's long-term arthritis. The painkillers that I've been stealing for at least the last six months.

I reach in and pick them up, feeling the packets shuffle easily around the space, hoping that Mum has already ordered more. A surge of disgust hits me, the same way it usually does. I push through it, knowing it'll only come back again but living for the ignorant moment. Some days, I can convince myself that this is fine, that I'm fine. Most days though, I'm well aware that I'm a scumbag. A dreadful, thieving scumbag, with morals so loose they require both belt and braces. This isn't who I am. But, for the time being, it's what I am. And I really don't know where it will end. I push two tablets from the blister pack and swallow them instantly, knowing that their comforting might will start to blunt the edges before long. Then I weigh up the possibility of adding a few more to my stores for the rest of the day. I consider how many remain in each strip, and decide that two from the middle and two from the back probably won't be missed.

They're in my pocket before my conscience has a word to say about it, and I quickly replace the leftovers, careful to position them exactly where they had been. The clock on the wall reminds me that I've barely been in our semi-detached family home for four minutes and I've managed to let down my parents, and further abuse my fragile body. The clock itself doesn't actually say all that, but I feel the judgement of its twenty-to-four frown pour down upon me.

Of course, these stolen pills aren't my only supply of solace: the chemists around Glasgow and the west of Scotland keep me topped up with over-the-counter stuff for in-between times. They aren't as strong, of course, but upping the dosage evens things out a bit. I've never hated myself more.

I keep a grotty cup in the car that I use to dissolve the soluble type in whatever liquid I have to hand – three-day-old water, cold tea from an old flask, and flat cola among the least nauseating. There's a plastic bottle in the bathroom cabinet at home for just the same purpose, and a mug beneath the bed, in case I stir during the night. I normally don't though, which is the main reason for the stockpile in the beside drawer that I throw down my throat before pulling the duvet over my tired head. There's enough anxiety puncturing my waking hours without having to cope with insomnia too.

I don't even know if they help any more; I feel just as fearful every minute and now I have an insatiable pet to feed too. Addiction is a beast with no master. I don't have any illusions really: I definitely have a problem. But, contrary to the internet's say-so, admitting it to myself didn't open up the path to recovery – it just gave me another reason to hate who I've become, and reinforced the need to hide more often from its reality. Throw another co-codamol on the barbie. The funny thing is – if funny even exists any more – I would never consider taking illegal drugs. Not even one, I'd be far too scared of their effects on my already delicate chemical make-up. But 38 different Big Pharma concoctions? Sure, I don't have anything else to do for the next 15 minutes. Can I take those to go?

I lock the front door and skulk back to the car, knowing that the short journey home will be just long enough for the painkillers to help me forget what a hideous excuse for a daughter I am. At least until the next time.

PAULA, THE LIAR

Living with myself has never come easily. I think it's one of the universe's best pranks: sticking me with a constant companion that most days I'd like to throw down a well, then making me scared of the water at the bottom. I guess that everyone has issues with ego at one point or another though. Being comfortable in one's own skin is only for those whose skin doesn't crawl at the sight of themselves. Mine catches a glimpse in the mirror and starts scuttling for the door.

Wait. Before you start to think that this isn't exactly the attitude you'd expect from a book on my recovery, please believe that I'm telling you all this precisely because of my recovery. It isn't every day, nor every week, in fact, that I feel like my own enemy, but I won't deny that sometimes, those past hurts creep back. I won't ever deny it again because – and here's the confession – I'm no longer ashamed of my mental health, and I won't allow myself to be convinced that I have to feel certain things at certain times in order to be an acceptable human.

Society is set up in such a way that it seems like nothing is more shameful than mental illness – except perhaps some of the most heinous crimes, and even then, the one is often blamed for the other. Lying about what was wrong with me became second nature. I'd never thought of myself as a liar, or a coward, or a thief. I always imagined I was one of those "good people" that you hear about; so scared was I of putting a foot out of place that I wouldn't even risk a toe on the neighbour's grass.

If I've learnt anything over the last few years though, it's that no one is inherently good or bad: not even Voldemort. Only how we respond to, and act upon, any given situation can define who we are at that very moment. Continuing that action, whatever it may be, will continue to define you. Unless you're a Disney princess, who has standards to uphold and a merchandising manager to please, you can be sure that, at some point, the righteous path will veer to the right when all you can do is wrong.

Anxiety didn't turn me into a liar, but it did cause me to lie. I did the rest.

LIES I TOLD TO COVER UP MY MENTAL HEALTH PROBLEMS

- There's something in my eye.
- I don't eat on Tuesdays. It's a religious thing. But I'll take a bit of that chocolate cake back to my car anyway.
- The invitation must have gone missing. Our postman isn't the most reliable.
- Oh, the shaking? I'm just really cold. Yes, I know it's summer. I have thin blood.
- It's not a twitch; it's called facial yoga.
- I don't celebrate Christmas. It's a non-religious thing. But I'll take a bit of that chocolate cake back to my car anyway.
- I'm not sure what happened there. I've never been like that before. Maybe it's a bug or something.
- I just don't like sports; I'm not scared of them.
- No, I always breathe this quickly. It's good for the complexion. Just let me sit down for a minute.
- I have a bit of a headache. Do you have any painkillers?
- I don't need to pee. We've only been out for eight hours.
- There's something in my other eye.
- Paula can't come to the phone at the moment. If you'd like to leave your name and number, she'll get back to you.
- The car just spun out of control ...

PAULA, THE RECKLESS

I grip the steering wheel so tightly that I'm leaving an impression. It's probably not a good one, knowing me. Even if I could loosen off, I'd never be able to make the impact that other people do. I just don't have it in me, and I'm on my way to prove that once again.

Red light. Phew. A moment's pause, physically at least. My mind whirs busily on.

It's only ever a 10-minute drive to the university building, but I'm sure the time is travelling much more quickly this morning, in spite of the rush-hour traffic. The car knows I don't want to get there and it's punishing me. I probably deserve it; there's so much grime on the windscreen it could start a new UK dance scene.

I promise I'll wash you, if you just break down, right here, and don't take me any further towards this tutorial. With wax and everything, and those little chamois cloths. Just break the hell down. Please!

The lights change and I press the accelerator optimistically, but all that breaks is my every hope and dream. The churning in my belly is no longer something I notice day-to-day, but since it has climbed up the Saffir–Simpson hurricane wind scale overnight, I'm suffering. I haven't properly eaten over the weekend because I knew this upheaval was coming, and the only thing worse than a group presentation, is a group presentation with an impromptu toilet break. It's worth the light-headedness to at least know digestion can't fail me now, although just the thought of it is turning my stomach.

Maybe the car park will be full, and I'll be late and miss our time slot. Or the other two members of my group will miraculously forget to turn up. But then, would I be made to present the entire assignment on my own? They couldn't do that, could they? I only know my part of the speech and, even then, I'll probably forget half of it when I'm standing up there, in front of everyone.

My knuckle cracks loudly against the wheel, and I can feel the tension of holding on with the might of the terrified moving up my arm. Just calm down. Breathe. But I can't, and I don't know why I bother even trying. Focusing on my breath, when all it's doing is continually speeding up, makes me think I'm dying. Am I dying? Maybe I am dying. If I died, I wouldn't have to ... oh, for God's sake, Paula, what an awful thing to think. It's a 10-minute presentation. Just go and do it. Nobody in the room will care what you're saying. You're in the fourth year of an accounting degree, giving a talk about an organisation's funding structure; it's not exactly a sell-out show. Polish up your backbone, for once, girl.

There are nine students in this Monday class – eight of whom know exactly what they're doing – and a tutor who I would imagine wears floor-length Dalmatian fur in her spare time. We've put in all the work for the assessment, including a misguided research trip to Aberfeldy one very icy Wednesday, and the written paper has come together well. But I know that the instant I open my mouth to explain the financial composition of our chosen charity to the assembled handful, only last night's tea will tumble out instead. I just can't face public speaking, even when that public is so small in number. They'll all be looking, waiting, expecting, and then, just like when Gran cheered the skater that slid out of his perfect spin to land forehead first on the ice, when I fall, they'll remember it forever, and bring it up every time there's a lull in conversation.

I release the brake and trundle onwards, almost but not quite at my destination. The motorway junction on my right looks so tempting right now. I could just slip away for the day and deal with the consequences later. The judgement of my group consequences, the failing the assignment consequences, the grubby self-loathing consequences. I keep going. As does the constant tirade of abuse and insults my brain is raining down upon me.

You cannot do this. You'll make a fool of yourself. You're going to fail anyway. You've always been a useless waste of too much flesh. I dig a fist into the roll of flab around my waist in agreement.

I'm convinced. I can't go to the presentation. I just can't. It's too much. I'm not strong enough and I can't face letting everyone else see how weak I really am.

I wait for a quiet side street and turn in, pulling off the busy main road, making sure there's no one around to see my meltdown.

This is the only thing I can do, I'm absolutely sure of it now.

Slowing down a little on approach, I bump the car onto the pavement and steer immediately towards the nearest lamppost, avoiding the instinct to slam on the brake. The bumper crunches, the headlight smashes, and I rest my head back against the seat, satisfied for the briefest of seconds, before the utter misery of another failure crushes me once again.*

PAULA, THE MASOCHIST

'Three people died today when a bomb ...'

That's as far into any news bulletin as I could ever manage before the guilt of inactivity rained down upon me. I was basically wet and miserable for about 20 years. For most of my life, I forced myself to sit through every summary and flash of bad news, immersing myself in the details so as not to hide from the fact that terrible things were happening in the world, and I wasn't helping. I'm pretty sure the behaviour would come under the "cruel and unusual punishment" heading, but surely if I let myself off with ignoring such horrors just because they upset me, I'd be as inhuman as those committing them. On top of just dragging myself through every gelatinous moment of each exhausting day then, I poured the world's tragedy into the mix and brought my forward momentum to a sticky end.

* After a good five minutes of tears, I waved away the two concerned onlookers and walked back home. The rest of my group presented without me, and thankfully passed. I was issued with a make-up assessment for my class and a hefty repair bill for my car. Until now, I've never admitted it wasn't an accident.

Please don't think me callous, but sometimes, I'm convinced, our processors just can't take any more input than we're already ingesting. And while volunteering and donating and campaigning was what kept my conscience from quickly killing me, I can't honestly say I was acting from anything outside my own emotional need. Big or small, life's problems affected me in a way that I can neither explain nor fully understand. I took every piece of information to its very unnatural conclusion; blowing things so far out of proportion, they needed a railcard to get back.

Let me give you an example. When you type the wrong word in a document and want rid of it, you just delete it and start again, right? I felt so ashamed of the waste of electricity and energy in that process – waste that was surely contributing to climate change and resource depletion – that I would only delete the letters I definitely didn't need, wherever they were in the word, and replace them alone. A tiny overreaction, maybe, but one of many that merged together to form constant, nagging self-reproach. The trouble was, I could never detach myself from responsibility for every wrong, and not only was it necessary for me get involved, but to feel the pain of the situation too. Because to escape the pain would surely be washing my hands of other people's hardships.

Logically, I knew I wasn't to blame for all the violence and suffering in the big, scary world, but that didn't mean I wasn't implicated, even if I was 13 years old with no functioning skills in international diplomacy. If you're not part of the solution, Paula ...

Every issue – of a close friend or a distant civilisation – became my own. It was felt with the same depth of emotion and dealt with equally as badly. Now, of course, I can see how much anxiety was tricking me into a trip of guilt that was so misguided it was off the map. And worthless too, in all honesty.

What good did my panic do for world hunger, or my tears for that poor, lost soul?

PAULA, THE KILLER

I splash cold water on my face then rest my wrists beneath the tap's cooling stream to calm a thumping pulse. It's been that kind of day. It's been the only kind of day lately. It's August, and the weather resembles summer in a way that Scotland never normally does. Pasty torsos and goose-bumped legs have been on show since the first crack of sunshine on Tuesday, and won't be hidden away until the temperature drops at least below brass monkeys. We're nothing if not opportunistic around these parts.

I am not a fan of the warm weather. It makes me flustered and sticky and breathless. I worry that sweat stains will highlight my constant discomfort, even though I'm always so cold they would likely turn to ice before soaking in. Summer, to me, is just winter without the layers of woolly armour.

But I do love how much the blue-sky days cheer other people. I spent 10 minutes at lunchtime watching how happy a group of mothers and their kids looked, just to be sitting on the grass, without wellies, or waterproofs, or wind-beaten faces. A little of their simple pleasure filtered through to me and, for a moment or two, I understood.

Now, back home, the front door is locked to the water-gun battles and after-work loungers. Gerry is back, the blinds are closed, and I can finally catch my breath. I perch on the edge of the bath, and drips from my chin fall down my dress. Reaching for a towel, I hear the daddy long legs flitting against the tiles before I see it. Up in the corner, typically, out of reach, and with no apparent intention of finding its own way out; bumping carelessly against the wall and ceiling in turn.

I've never been scared of insects or spiders. I am scared of hurting them, just as I'm scared of hurting anything, but so often inadvertently do. When I was about six, I spent a few weeks walking only on my tiptoes, as I had just learnt about dust mites in school and couldn't bear to step on one – accidentally or otherwise.

I shout for Gerry to bring in a glass from the kitchen, hoping to catch this gangly fellow and release him out of the window: the daddy long legs, not Gerry, who is neither gangly, nor fond of being released from windows.

With the towel wound tightly in my hand, I clamber into the bath and try wafting air towards our guest, to coerce him to move. He only shuffles then re-settles, further away than before. Gerry has brought in the glass and asks if I'd prefer him to establish the rapport with our eight-legged visitor, but I'm determined I can rescue it. I just need to get closer ...

Carefully, I step up onto the lip of the bath, hold the towel over my shoulder and, aiming far enough to the left to be completely non-threatening, whip the towel against the wall.

Thwump.

The towel falls back into my hand. I look up. It moved. But I can't see it. Where did it go? I spin towards Gerry. His face is scrunched in concern. I follow his gaze towards the plughole, where two needle-thin black lines stand out against the white plastic. A foot away, the remainder of the little broken body rests.

Oh no. Oh God. I can't believe this. I was just trying to help. This can't have happened.

But it has.

I killed it.

I've been crying on the bathroom floor for about 10 minutes. In between efforts to console me, Gerry has removed both parts of the body, out of my line of vision. I'm shaking violently, and I can't stop thinking that I've plucked a life out of the air. I didn't mean to, but does that even matter? Those were my fingers holding the towel, my clumsy decisions that put me up there, too close to become anything other than a killer. What if this affects the eco system? Is that even possible? Either way, I've robbed a fellow creature of all it had in store, and that's not something I'll ever accept easily.

I know it will take a while to calm myself down from this one but, right at this moment, I don't think I ever deserve to feel better anyway.

THINGS PEOPLE UNDERSTAND BETTER THAN SOCIAL ANXIETY

- Quantum mechanics.
- Mumblers.
- Why *My So-Called Life* was cancelled after that epic first series.
- Every physical health condition.
- How anyone can still imagine that the earth is flat. I'm no geographer but I haven't fallen off the world once.
- Double taxation. I spent a year grasping this concept for the briefest of seconds, then losing it almost as quickly.
- The special rules for personal space on public transport.
- Teenagers.
- The correct use of apostrophes and the fact that the sign-writer's proofreading fee should always be paid.
- Whether they're going to be late or early the day after the clocks go back.
- That sometimes it's better just to be quiet.

CHAPTER 7

ADVENTURES INCOMING

'Happy birthday, Paula!' Gerry smiles so warmly as I open my 30-year-old eyes that my retinas almost burn. Today, as he so astutely announces, is my birthday – and happy? I guess, I must be.

We've managed to escape the flat. Last night – under the cover of winter darkness – we drove up to a hotel in rural Perthshire; one of my favourite places in the world. It's quiet and calming, with so few people around that I can normally go outside unnoticed.

Gerry shrewdly stocked up on snacks so there was no pressure for me to leave the room at all, once we had negotiated check-in. I did manage a quick walk around the sprawling grounds though, without seeing a soul, in spite of the bright moonlight. There's a birthday card by the bed; its gold envelope making me think of a glitzy awards ceremony.

And the award for least functioning 30-year-old goes to ...

My name is on the inside, with some beautiful words I don't deserve, from a husband who, for a reason I have yet to figure out, seems to think I'm worth all this ridiculous effort. Maybe it's all a long con – a really long con – and one day he'll run off with all the money I don't actually have. I often think about how I'd react and, honestly, along with the utter heartbreak and devastation that would crush my entire universe, I think I'd feel a tiny bit relieved. Relieved, not that I'd lost the only person I can always bear to be around, but that I no longer had to worry myself sick about losing him. I'm sure my anxiety must make him miserable, although he'd never say. All those evenings going over and over the very minutiae of my days, talking me down from the ledge of overreaction and panic; the time spent planning for every exaggerated eventuality, the distance gone to scout out each next step.

Having anxiety is exhausting. Loving someone with anxiety doesn't look like much more fun. From the second my head and pillow go their separate ways each morning, I'm jumping through the misshapen hoops of my coping strategies. The first, of course, is medication. The next depends on what kind of day I'm staring down the barrel at.

Today, my 30th birthday, is a special kind of hell all of its own, and I just don't have the blueprint for this one. It's Saturday; the best day for a birthday, so I'm told. But I can't help but think that's only the case if you enjoy those special little things, like spending time with other people and being alive. 'Let's just go down for breakfast. It might be quiet.' I nod. 'Do you want to just stay here?'

I nod. 'All day?'

I let my head thump back against the wall. It's uncomfortable but I don't recognise comfort anyway.

I don't want to feel like this. I'm officially 30 years old. Surely I should have it all sussed by now. 30 doesn't look like this in films. 30 looks confident, and enlightened, and secure. If I could force myself to look in the mirror right now, I wouldn't see any of those things. I'm not 30; I'm two terrified 15-year-olds, ripping each other apart for the best hiding place.

I'm so lucky, I keep trying to remind myself. And so disgustingly ungrateful for not being able to enjoy it. But the thought of leaving this safe, warm room and venturing out to God-knows-what beyond that door, fills me with the kind of fear that no horror film can conjure.

Gerry picks up my book and lays it on the bed beside me. I've no idea how but, for someone who has never had any issues with mental health, he understands that I don't mean to be so damned awkward about everything. I just can't seem to find another way.

Maybe we'll go outside later, take a trip to the local village and buy cake in celebration. Or stroll around that park I've always admired from the road. I shut my eyes again, as Gerry shuffles his arm around my shoulders.

How did I get to this point?

And, more importantly, how will I ever get past it?

EUREKA!

As much as I love a good exclamation, there wasn't actually an Archimedes moment when adventure displaced anxiety in my soggy psyche. Neither did I sit bolt upright in bed one morning, with all the answers set out just waiting to be practically applied. Three decades of social anxiety, panic, and depression are not, I assure you, ready to give up their hold without the fight of a lifetime. So far, I'd never been strong enough to even find my way into the ring.

By my late twenties, I was so far from recovery that I couldn't afford the air fare back. Pills to help me face the night, followed by pills to help me face the day, and the panic attacks were so close together that I could touch one from the other. Not only were cold callers not welcome at my door, I wouldn't even answer the bell to warm callers any more. On a good day, I would make it to work with some tears, and make it back with some tissues. On a bad day, both tears and tissues were used up at home. Just the admin of being an adult was too much for my chaotic filing system, and after the five-day breakdown that had taken me to the edge of reason, those guys with "THE END IS NIGH" signs had started to look kinda hopeful.

Around the same time, I'd been visiting my doctor regularly – as all crazy people are wont to do – and everyone involved had realised that we weren't making progress. I wasn't particularly deteriorating – I'm not sure there were any depths left to plumb – I just wasn't improving any either. As far as the professionals were concerned, I was pretty much being my best self: as pathetic as that self was. We could vary the dosage, if I really wanted, or go all the way back to A in *The Big Book of Drugs* and start over again. But perhaps the life that I had was just the most I could ever expect from myself. Psychiatry had decided their services weren't appropriate, and the only other option on the table was time in hospital. And that was a table I wasn't sure I was ready to sit down at just yet.

Of course, I had also just turned 30. Not that the number itself affected me in any great way. I'm not Count von Count. But as my fourth decade began, I was reminded that three had passed without note or novelty. What had happened to that five-year-old girl who was convinced she would one day right the world's wrongs? Or at least write them. There I was, as grown-up as I was ever going to be, and I couldn't even right myself, never mind the rest of humanity. It's hard to see a new way for society, when your outlook stops just short of your tenement walls. I had never lost the will to give something to the world, I'd just lost the belief that I had anything worth giving.

Surely this wasn't it? This couldn't be all that I was, all that I ever would be. There had to be another way forwards for me; if only I could find it. If only someone could teach me to see it.

I started to look again, not aggressively or with any great purpose; there were no spreadsheets or wall-charts, and I don't even remember consciously deciding to up my research game. It was just a continuation really of 20 years of hoping for a cure – any cure – to drag me from the ditch onto the green. I did make a list of all the treatments and avenues I had already tried, much like the one on page 67. The intention was, I guess, to find a gap, something I hadn't given my complete attention to, or exhausted to its fullest potential.

Instead I noticed a pattern; well, more of a lack of a pattern. In all those searches to find someone, anyone, to help ease my mental turmoil, I had trusted doctors and counsellors, the strange and the stranger, any crank who had bothered to post a decent review online. But I had never trusted the one person who knew my every struggle, from the inside out.

Over the years, I had somehow learnt that I was not to be trusted, that my decisions and opinions were worth less than everyone else's. Only outsiders could comment on, or support, my mental health. After all, it was my mind that was causing all the problems; how could I rely on its output to save me?

When I looked back over the list though, only three difficult choices were available:

1. Request a hospital bed.
2. Continue with my 40+ pills a day regime, until those steadily worsening pains in my arms and chest brought the situation to a quiet close.
3. Give myself a chance. Could I, for once, put a little faith in myself to find a way out? And, if I could, did I have the strength to walk through that door, no matter how terrifying the other side?

As I said, "eureka" never came, but what did come was the resolve. Without ever really meaning to, I had decided: if the end for my mental health journey was nigh, I was going to be the one holding the banner.

PART TWO
THE ADVENTURE

CHAPTER 8

ADVENTURES IN SPORT

Paula must try harder to take part.

Paula must try harder to remember her kit.

Paula must try harder to attend classes.

As if Paula wasn't trying hard enough just to make it through "the best days of my life," my high school P.E. teachers could never find anything to write on my report cards other than that I should be making more effort. Granted, I didn't give them much to work with, since my forged notes turned up to P.E. more than I ever did. But still, did the "uninterested, no application" checkbox have to be ticked every single time?

Just in case I haven't made it painfully clear already, growing up, I was never very sporty. Sports required agility and strength and coordination, and, above all, they required the confidence to risk falling on your face in front of a crowd. I had the falling bit down pat. But add in the crowd and I wanted to keep falling for eternity and never resurface. Particularly when that crowd consisted of 40 teenagers in branded active-wear who could smell inadequacy across a packed gym hall.

From an early age, anxiety robbed me of physical activity but, in all truth, I didn't really feel like a victim of this particular crime. I wasn't exactly mourning the loss of a potential athletics career. Sport held no interest for me anyway; anxiety could have this one. Of course, anxiety wouldn't just stop there. If it had, we would probably have got along just fine. I could do without muscle definition, if it could let me have social skills. Instead it took more and more, right down to my very last friendship, and when the time came to either sink beneath its might, or finally learn to swim, well, you see where this cliché is going.

In case you can't, however, I'll tell you. The cliché is heading towards sport, and taking me with it. You see, I had come up with an idea ...

... One night when the London Olympics had somehow found its way onto our TV, I thought it would be hilarious if someone who had never tried a sport before tried all the sports. Fine, "hilarious" is a stretch, but imagine that one girl you know who has managed to get by without ever even tossing a coin, having to give the shot put a go. Of course, you probably can't imagine it, since there is no girl who hasn't tried her hand, foot or wits at one sport or another in all her days.

But there was. She was me.

The Commonwealth Games were heading for my city, almost a stone's throw from my home – if you throw stones better than I do – and I was uniquely placed to test each of the 17 sports as an absolute beginner.

The whole thing seemed perfect, except that I really didn't want to do it. This challenge had all the elements that anxiety used against me: people, the outdoors, water, activity, potential for failure, more people. The fear could finally break me. Or it could be my one last chance to break the fear. I had to take it.

Gerry set up the blog, knowing that my fondness for the written word, and my fear of the judgement of others would help hold me to account, and spur me on.

So began my adventures in anxiety. And so began Paula Must Try Harder.

THE GLASGOW 2014 CHALLENGE

[From the blog – August 2012]

What?

To progress as far as possible from a standing (probably more like kneeling) start in each of the 17 Commonwealth sports. As a complete novice, I don't expect to set the sporting world alight but, if there's an award for turning up, trying hard and embarrassing oneself mightily, I'll be on that podium crying my tired wee eyes out in no time.

Why?

Sport is for all; beginners welcome; you can do it!

I've chuckled cynically at such quotes from sports clubs and health departments all my life. There's no way someone as uncoordinated, bookish, and bungling as me could pick up a sport after avoiding physical exercise into adulthood. I've decided to prove myself right – or become an athletic goddess.

Win – win.

When?

Before the Games reach Glasgow in 2014, so less than two years to sample 17 sports. I haven't thought this through.

Where?

Anywhere that'll take me. Probably just in my house then.

How?

Through hard work, effort, and blogging! Help keep me motivated by reading about my attempts, joining in with the games, and sharing my challenge with everyone you know who has any interest (or none) in sport and its newest ~~runner~~, ~~swimmer~~, ~~jumper~~, ~~bowler~~, trier.

CYCLING

I need to start somewhere, and I've watched kids learn to ride a bike on our street in less than an hour, so it seemed like an easy win from the list. Plus, unless you're playing the bicycle-built-for-two angle, cycling is a wonderfully solitary sport and, for a sociophobe, that's the biggest pro a sport can have in its column.

This was the plan:

1. Buy a bike.
2. Force myself out to the back garden.
3. Ride the bike.
4. Declare cycling a success.

The first two steps worked well, considering. I managed to go bike shopping, although I probably should have agreed to actually sit on the saddle in the store, to test the fit for my height, like Gerry recommended. I've never been able to try anything on in shops though, and I don't just mean because of the communal changing rooms and judgy shop assistants. Even items as innocuous as scarves or sunglasses are taken home, untried, because the thought of wearing something, even momentarily, in a public area, without vetting how stupid it looks first is unbearable.

The salesman clearly knew a thing or two about cycling and was determined to pass on at least five of them to me, while I just wanted to be back home already, cooing happily over the only outdoor equipment I'd ever owned. Cycling was an activity I was meant to be able to do by myself, yet here I was, being engaged forcibly in conversation before I could even congratulate myself on my biggest sporting triumph to date. Luckily, Gerry can spot my discomfort from space, and knows enough about derailleurs to keep a cycling chat on track. So, we eventually escaped with a bike I could only hope I would bond with, and some great advice on buying my next one.

After that, all I had to do was take said bike out to the garden one dry afternoon. Easy? Not easy. For two main reasons. In Scotland, a dry afternoon is like a kumquat: everyone is sure they've had one, but no one can quite remember when. And when the drizzle finally does stop, it's not likely that the meteorological timings will line up with my own good weather days. It's amazing just how many excuses a person – not naming names – can concoct for not going outside to make a complete fool of herself ... or himself. Gerry, quite hopefully, has been leaving my bike (now named Bella) in the hall, since I'll surely be using it too much to move it further from the front door. Also, tripping over the tyres on my way to the bathroom might become annoying enough to force the issue. Something to note though, annoyance ranks a distant second to social phobia, and I could probably have lasted another month or so of scuffing my ankles on the gears every time I went for a pee, as long as I didn't have to face the potential of someone seeing me failing to ride a bike.

I did manage to make it downstairs with the bike once. Not outside though. As soon as I spotted all those windows, with the threat of neighbours leaning against their glass, I was reminded that I had invoices to be getting on with, or something. That familiar disappointment rumbled around in my gut as Bella and I clattered back up to the flat. Clearly, the garden was far too close to home for my first lesson so, last weekend, we loaded the bike into the car and drove down the coast, and around the coast, and further along the coast, looking for the *perfect* spot for me to conquer my first sport.

It took three hours of our Saturday to realise that there was no spot on this island perfect enough to convince me to pedal my way out of my comfort zone. Every path or promenade we passed, Gerry pointed out the level surface, the lack of spectators, while I talked myself further into my own headspace. He loves cycling and can't wait until I do too, which he's certain will happen the second I freewheel down a hill. But that would require some real improvement on my current stats.

Number of times on a bike: 1.

Number of times actually moving on a bike: 0.

On the despondent drive back, I fell into my usual spiral of self-loathing: despondent, ashamed, and uncommunicative. We had a brief conversation somewhere around Ayrshire that started with one of us saying, 'What the hell is wrong with me?'

And the other saying, 'If you're going to try 17 sports, Paula, you're going to have to try one.'

That's why I'm currently sitting outside a cycling centre for the third time this week, trying not to allow myself to turn the car around again and head home. Logically, I absolutely know that the good people inside won't laugh at me or make me wear the losers' helmet for my entire visit. I'm pretty sure they teach adults to cycle all the time, even though in all the hours I've been creepily watching, only toddlers and their grown-ups have used the learners' track.

All I have to do is just make this first move: walk over and ask for help.

I can do it. And I will.

Tomorrow.

THREE WEEKS LATER

This time. I've even parked closer so I don't have as far to change my mind on the walk over.

Last night, I made the decision to write on the blog that I would be taking a cycling lesson today. No one reads it, I'm sure, but it doesn't matter. Just putting it up there was enough. The burden of social anxiety might also be the only thing that can persuade me to push myself beyond it. Now that I've announced to the world – okay, to the webmaster – that I'm learning to ride a bike, there's no way I can do anything else. I couldn't bear to have to say I failed or, worse, wasn't able to try. Of course, I haven't admitted that I'm struggling with my mental health; as far as the blog is concerned, I'm just a clumsy idiot trying out all the sports for the first time. And maybe, for today, that's something I can at least attempt to be.

My feet are shaking, but they're still moving me somewhat steadily towards the park. I didn't know feet could shake, but apparently they can – and mine are quite proficient. There are walkers milling around and I'm tempted to just meander off myself, but I stick to the path, and my plan, and soon I'm beside the little cycle track, catching the eye of the woman in hi-vis and helmet, who seems to be just finishing up with an after-school-club session.

She smiles, and I return what I hope looks like a smile, but what feels like a crazed grimace. It doesn't seem to put her off though, as she joins me on the grass. Maybe that face is common to cyclists; they are often heading into the wind. Without giving myself time to think, I explain that I emailed a few weeks back, asking if I could pop down sometime for a lesson, apologising that work has kept me from visiting sooner. (Otherwise known as lying.) I'm almost positive that the instructor has passed me more than a few times while I've been on my daily vigil in the next street along, but she's polite enough not to mention it.

In fact, maybe it isn't politeness, maybe it's just ruthless efficiency because before I've even decided if I'm staying, she's lowering the saddle on a nearby mountain bike and beckoning me to try it out. With a few quick glances around to make sure the youngsters aren't looking in my direction, I clamber onto the saddle and try to ignore the thumping of blood through my veins that's making me feel like I might pass out. Just keep it together for one lesson and I promise you never have to come back.

After a few safety tips that sound like Charlie Brown's teacher to my stressed ear canals, the coach edges me onto the track and encourages me to just give it a go.

I fall off. I get back on.

I fall off again. I almost get back on then notice a passer-by not passing by quite quickly enough and I stop. I think it's time to go home.

THE FOLLOWING WEEK

My instructor has taken off the pedals and I'm paddling along the track with my feet on the concrete, like a two-year-old on a balance bike. There's a two-year-old on a balance bike at the opposite end of the path. She's loving life. I'm not loving her. She's making it look easy, in a way that only the very young can. I know it's because she has no sense of failure, or danger, or even time. She'll get there when she gets there and that's all she needs to know. I am getting nowhere – either fast or with an ounce of self-respect. Every couple of yards, I lose concentration, drawn back inside my head, where only judgement and insecurity lie. The skills aren't coming easily because I've never had to learn anything like this before, and I'm so busy trying to override all I know about myself that it's hard to just know how to ride.

But I'm here, back at the scene of last week's defeat, and that's achievement enough right now. I spent a few days unsure that I could cope with another try at this bizarre set of interconnected movements that seem to come so naturally to all but me.

Yesterday, a teenager wheelied past me down the street, while talking on his phone. I still don't know which brake to press so that I don't go over the handlebars. It seemed like I just wasn't meant for this strange, complicated world.

Then, just for a moment or two, I allowed myself to feel something that I haven't in such a long time: pride. It was fleeting, and hard to recognise at first, but it was there.

Cycling is the only thing I've ever tried that I don't know what the outcome will be. Sure, I've been to university and faced plenty of academic and life challenges, but I already knew that I had what it would take to succeed there, as long as I just put in the work. Here, in this park, though, I've no idea if I'll ever manage to move the pedals at the right time and hold the handlebars just where I should to make this contraption go where I want it to. Even if I do, will I ever be consistent enough to be able to call what I'm doing cycling? I really don't know.

Yet still, I keep trying. My legs are bruised from knee to ankle. I have scrapes the lengths of my hands and wrists. My nerves are in pieces. And I'm trying.

A bright light flashes from the not-too-distant distance, and I remember that Gerry is hiding – bravely – in the bushes, taking photos, because I still won't let him near me with a camera. He's insistent that I need the visuals for the blog, so I've allowed the sneaky picture-taking, as long as he doesn't get himself arrested.

The camera flashes again. I stop. We go home.

TWO MONTHS DOWN THE ROAD

I'm riding a bike! I'm riding a bike!

This is incredible. I've never felt so free in all my life.

A car park at the foot of the Ochil hills is the venue for my first cycling success. My instructor advised me just to keep practising and, since I'm still too self-conscious to do so in the park 100 metres from my home, we've brought the bikes out to Stirlingshire, where I know absolutely no one, so am guaranteed to meet them.

There's nothing different about today. I'm wearing the same inappropriate cycling clothing – a dress and ballet pumps – as every other time we've come out. Gerry has been doing laps of the little green, careful not to watch me, but still keeping an eye out. Bella and I have been falling over for at least an hour so far; every time both feet have found the pedals, I've veered to the edge of the path, wobbled, and tumbled onto the damp grass. It had been a fairly frustrating morning, and we were making our way back to the car when it seemed that little square of parking spots might be the perfect place for one last run. Not so narrow that I could topple off its edge, not so littered that I could become fixated and steer towards an obstacle.

It didn't happen at once. Or at twice. But at thrice, I'm going, in the same direction as the bike, at a rate of nought – but still faster than I've ever gone before. The grin won't leave my daft face and Gerry is laughing, maybe at me, but I don't care. The wind whips my hair across my forehead. I still can't seem to turn right, but left is all I need for now.

I'm riding a bike. For the first time, as a 31-year-old woman. And I'm beyond excited.

Thump ...

I rode a bike!

TAKING A LEAP

I read somewhere that rockets have to expend 90 per cent of their fuel just to leave the launch pad. It's probably an urban myth – or a rural one, for all I know – but the figure really struck me.

That's exactly what it feels like to attempt anything with anxiety.

The first step in any task is well known to be the biggest, but the architect really messed up the proportions when he added in anxiety. Even just forming a plan to go outside, or use the phone, seems so terrifyingly huge as to surely be insurmountable. And then, after the planning, there's the actual doing: that's if you have a crumb of space left in your already crammed thought-basket to even consider it. Normally, you don't. It's all just too much: too much could go wrong, too much could change, just too much.

That first step looms like a mountain above you, and you don't think you have the energy to climb it. But, as soon as you burn all that fuel and struggle your way up just that one step, the next seems a little bit less draining to take. Not to say though that it quickly became easy to override the anxiety. This ship didn't reach orbit until at least a few sports in, and even then, it wasn't a stable trajectory. I wobble off track often, even now, but I always know I can find my way back because I've already plotted the course. Trying the sports, testing myself against the fear, that was my launch pad.

In fact, I can pinpoint the episode that really started the turnaround for me. And, boy, was it an episode. During my second badminton lesson in a sports hall in Cumbernauld, a gaggle of teenagers burst onto the courts, giggling and jeering and generally just having a damn good time. Now, they were the kind of kids that played badminton of a weekend with their mates so I'm guessing they probably weren't out for blood, but from the second they arrived, I was right back in high school. They were laughing at me, I was sure of it. They could tell I didn't know what I was doing. My service wasn't exactly silver, and I couldn't string a rally together with a ball of twine. It was just like P.E. all over again.

Obviously, on reflection, those young folk had no interest in my existence. I wasn't even on their radar – or whatever app they use for that these days. To them, I was just an old dear creaking around the gym, moving so slowly their sharp eyes didn't register the motion. They were only having a good time, but my perception was so skewed by anxiety that their Saturday game became all about me.

There's no other way to say that I completely lost my shit that afternoon. Tears and snot poured out of my face, as I stumbled, sobbing, off the court, in a scene all of my own making. If I had wanted everyone in the building to look at me, I couldn't have done a better job. It was truly pathetic, and the whole way home I cursed myself for being such a total loser. All I had to do was stay and face down what my anxiety was building in front of me. That time, I couldn't, but I was determined to never, ever let myself get into that same mess again.

Of course, that's not how it happened. There were plenty of other setbacks and crises; it was two years of sport with chronic anxiety – what did I expect? Most days I was a snivelling wreck. No, that's not what changed things. What changed things was the aftermath of that badminton incident: when I decided to admit to the world that I was struggling.

Back home, I asked Gerry to take a photo of my puffy, tear-ridden face, and I posted it on the blog, with an explanation of my mental health condition. I confessed, for the first time, that social anxiety was killing me, and that my Glasgow 2014 challenge wasn't just for laughs and chuckles. I was trying to save my own life. I'd never spoken publicly about my mental health; I never thought I would. It was no one's business and it couldn't possibly help. I would just be giving people another reason to think I was a failure. Now though, it felt important. Even if no one ever saw it, I had still been ready to put it out there, and that was enough.

But people did see it, and they responded. Not how I thought they would either. Nobody said that I was weak or self-obsessed; they didn't point fingers or poke at my wounds. All that they said – in outpourings of kindness – was that I was not alone. From that moment, I realised that my silly sports experiment was no longer just about me. The next day, when I received the message to say that I'd made it acceptable to go out and live with anxiety, or the following week when someone got in touch to talk about their agoraphobia, or two years later when a woman started swimming lessons because, no matter how scared she was, she could never be as scared as me, I was reminded that we're all just bumbling through the world as best we can.

Only some of us do it in Lycra.

TRIATHLON

My start wave is due to head off in less than a minute and I'm still not sure I'll actually be starting. I am in the water though, wearing my yellow cap and timing chip, and clinging on to the tiled edge, so it would seem to an outsider that I'm involved in this race.

Most of the other competitors in my grouping are perched eagerly at the poolside, ready to dive into the deep end to begin their 400m swim majestically. This initial section of the triathlon won't look quite as graceful the way I'll be doing it: holding on to a bright pink float, splashing and kicking from this end to that and back again, more times than I really want to think about. The distinct lack of floor beneath my feet is already stirring up a panic and my heart rate has increased to a frenzied drum solo. My knuckles tighten their grip on the side.

I don't know why I'm doing this. I can't swim. God knows I've tried. I've been going to lessons for months, even taking phobia sessions, but this is my first time beyond the safety of the shallow end and I think I might just die.

Suddenly, the rest of the line-up pounds into the pool and the surge of the water reminds me that I'm supposed to be moving too. There must have been a whistle or something, but all I've been able to hear for the last half-hour is my own ringing terror.

I let go of the edge, kick off gingerly and follow my float slowly down the lane. My eyes are closed behind my goggles and I haven't taken a breath. I think I'm crying. This is Length One. Once I reach the end of Length 16, I have the privilege of being allowed to clamber out of the water, and shuffle barefoot into the transition area to find my bike for a quick 10 km around the park.

Something to look forward to.

A volunteer jumps into the lane beside me because, I guess, she can see just how frightened I am. 'You can do this. You're almost there.'

Her confidence makes up for my lack, and I keep struggling on. My head, as usual, is working against me, convincing me that this is the worst idea I've ever had. It's probably right. I'm not even a third done, and people who I'm trying really hard to ignore are already leaping out with more energy than I had at the start.

I should be mortified – taking part in a triathlon with a stupid big float – but I'm too tired to feel anything above basic functions. I suppose there's probably an element of determination in here too, but I couldn't point to it.

Yet here I am, still going, legs aching and lungs burning, about to finish my swim, just as the next wave is limbering up to make their start. I'm last out but I don't care; at least I'm out.

The cycle is passing in a blur. Not for everyone watching, I'm sure, although I do manage the hills with less strain than I expected on my gazelle of a road bike, Nancy. I'm moving pastel hair bobbles from one dropped handlebar to the other after each lap, in order that I don't lose count, as I've been warned of the dreaded "Did Not Finish" if I miss one of the seven circuits. The wet fabric of my tri-suit clings to my thighs and I'm constantly reminded to be embarrassed, in front of all these strangers who have gathered around the park's paths to cheer us on and ... I'm not embarrassed. Around every corner there are more eyes to watch as I puff and wheeze and, yes, fall off once or twice, on my way to the second transition point, and I don't care. In fact, I wave and even smile, as they witness my wobbly legs power me on my way.

My left knee is scuffed and a little bloody. I'm not sure I can straighten my fingers. Maybe I'll just have claws now. But I'm not stopping. Just one more bobble to move and I'm there. One more time over that hill. I hear my name and turn my head, just in time to see my friend Tess, waving from the sidelines. She's standing with my family, all laughing, and for just a moment I wonder what they're laughing at – or who. The bike wiggles a little beneath me, as though to remind me what I'm here for, and I realise that those wonderful folk who have turned up to lend me their support aren't taking the piss out of me. That's anxiety talking, trying to derail my attempts to move past it.

I press down harder on the pedals.

Someone hands me a plastic cup of water and I stop to take a drink, ignoring the shouts to keep going. I just need a bloody minute, people. I reckon I'm about three kilometres in, with only one left to suffer, and, since I'm not exactly aiming for gold here, I'm having a moment's pause, whether that's in the rules or not. Running is not in my playbook. I'd go so far as to say I dislike running. I want to love it, like all the inspirational quotes online tell me I should, but I don't. There's no buzz or endorphin rush; just panting, and sweating, and joint pain, with the occasional glimpse of hope that something might trip me up, so I can have a lie down for a little while. I've really made the effort to bond with running, but we just don't get along. Somewhere, about 12 furlongs in front of me, is my training partner, Helen, who is the main reason I've managed to clock up as many miles over the months as I have. The thought of joining her for a cake* once all this is over spurs me on, and that promise of sugar convinces my muscles to pick up the pace for just a little while longer.

And there it is: the end. I can see it as I turn back into the park. Music is playing, and spectators line the path, and I'm nearly there. I'm too exhausted to worry what everyone else is thinking about my shoddy performance or jiggling hind-end.

Just a few more steps.

The announcer calls my name as I cross the line: Paula "Must Try Harder" McGuire.

Dad is in tears. A medal is dropped around my neck; its weight comforting against my chest.

* Cake has always featured heavily in my diet but, by this point, I could even eat it in public - as long as I had broken it down into crumbs first. (In case you were wondering.)

I'm a triathlete. I'm still scared of water. I've only just learnt to ride a bike. I've never run before in my life.

But I'm a triathlete, and now there's nothing I can't try.

AND THE REST …*

Weightlifting: Three sessions with an Olympian and several members of the Scottish Commonwealth team taught me that I'm not a natural lifter of heavy things, particularly when I was first handed the children's bar and promptly fell over. But I did learn how to perform a decent Clean and Jerk, and a passable Snatch.

Personal best: Clean and Jerking 20kg. Personal worst: Laughing every time someone mentioned a big Snatch.

Aquatics: Being terrified of big puddles put me at a distinct disadvantage in the pool-based sports, and it took me several months of one-to-one lessons, my mum joining my group classes to hold my hand, and a long weekend with a phobia specialist in Manchester for me to finally brave the shallow end. Five years later and my front crawl no longer resembles a cat in a bath. My breaststroke still does.

Lawn bowls: The outright winner of the Most Versatile Sport award goes to this friendly or competitive, gentle or dynamic game, that I have now played with octogenarians, vegetarians and at least one seminarian. Before losing half his fingers, my dad was a trophy winner and, while I'm not quite following in his soft-shoed footsteps, my visits to Woodend Bowling Club are now among my favourite hours spent outdoors.

* The logistics of trying 17 sports was a challenge in itself, since I wasn't exactly practised in asking for help. After the first blog post or two though, clubs and athletes started to get in touch, inviting me along to give their sport a go. Slowly, I became adept at pestering the hell out of people until they eventually agreed that it would be truly wonderful to have me join them for an afternoon.

Athletics: Perhaps it wasn't my finest idea to take my first run and jump at track and field among 10-year-olds at a school athletics day. I'm quite sure the kids had more fun than I did, relaying faster, and shot putting farther than I ever could – and with plenty more skill. It did prepare me, however, for the ignominy of being overtaken in the walking marathon by a grandmother pushing a double buggy. She offered me a boiled sweet on her way past though.

Netball: My first team sport wasn't exactly a triumph, since I hadn't the slightest idea how to find a way into a squad that had already gelled better than a Teddy Boy, but after an hour or so of practising, I could certainly net a ball five times out of ten, as long as no one was defending. My ball skills, it seems, outweigh my people skills. Make of that what you will.

Table tennis: This sport schooled me above all else in diplomacy, since I spent an inordinate proportion of my time chasing the ball from my game across the tables of everyone else's. Great fun, and some excellent – and completely accidental – trick shots, punctuated by prolonged spells of crawling around the floor. All in all, a great way to spend an afternoon – and an old pair of tights.

Hockey: Hit a ball with a big stick: sounds straightforward. Hit a ball with a big stick while lots of other women run towards you with big sticks of their own: not quite so straightforward. These women were tough, and not afraid to use it. And I loved it. They taught me how to control the ball, how to shoot for goal, and, more than that, how to enjoy being as tough as I'd never imagined I could be.

Judo: Wearing an Olympic silver medallist's outfit, while said silver medallist watched her fellow Olympian husband teach me the basics of their sport was, without exaggeration, terrifying. Before long though, I was so caught up in the lessons, in the gentle ways of the discipline, and, I admit, in the joys of throwing an opponent onto a mat, I forgot to care who was looking on. That, right there, is the power of sport.

Wrestling: Meet Commonwealth silver medallist for first time. Be pinned to ground by Commonwealth silver medallist. Lie awkwardly on top of Commonwealth silver medallist, while he explains the wacky wrestling points system that means he's still winning this round. Try not to graze genitals - of either participant - on dismount. Shake hands with Commonwealth silver medallist. Avoid eye contact. Leave.

Gymnastics: Running off to the circus wasn't ever in my career plan, but when you're offered the chance to learn acrobatics with the local troupe, you find yourself accepting the invitation quicker than you can juggle your own life choices. With absolutely no prior gymnastics experience to my name, I wasn't entirely convinced the circus could make anything but a clown of me. But soon I was upside down, acro-balancing on my coach's upturned legs, which, if nothing else, is a nice way to spend a Saturday afternoon.

Boxing: As a lifelong pacifist, hitting someone repeatedly in the face isn't how I pictured myself making my mark. Luckily for me, I'm also slow and weak so there was no "face hitting" and certainly no "repeatedly" in my boxing repertoire. I gave a few punching bags a good going over though. I've since given cage fighting a go; it beat the peace right back into me.

Shooting: I had always hoped to make it through life without ever handling a firearm. Even toy guns make me uncomfortable. So, aiming a shotgun into the air, even at inanimate objects was a huge stretch of my character. What if that clay had a family? As soon as I felt the gun's recoil on my bruised shoulder and realised that I was the only one in any pain, the rest of the experience was guilt-free. I even hit a few. I'm sure they'd had a good, long life.

Squash: While 1980s suits in action films made squash look as clammy as a New England chowder, I rarely broke a sweat during my game with the Scottish champions. Not, of course, due to my superior fitness level or natural flair for smacking balls off walls, but because I spent so little time actually hitting anything. Running around in a glass-walled box did make me feel trapped in a sci-fi future though, so I can't complain. My advice: find someone who is as good / bad as you are at this sport before giving it a go or you'll quickly become the ball boy in your own game.

Rugby Sevens: The last of my 17 new sports is so fondly remembered, not only because it meant I could go home and sit down for the foreseeable. It was the Friday before the Glasgow 2014 Opening Ceremony – cutting it fine for my deadline, I know – and I was joining the Team Scotland men for one of their last training sessions before they played for their country – and mine – in the Games the following week. Somehow, the sun was shining over the pitches and, as my burly teammates hoisted me aloft to teach me something about a lineout, all I knew was that any sport in which such strong hands support my backside is one that I can get behind.

THINGS I LEARNT FROM SPORT

- How to do the perfect forward roll. (In theory.) In practice, I barely managed a half-assed sideways effort.
- That people who do sport as adults are not the same people who do sport as kids. I was fully prepared to be bullied for throwing too short or standing still too long. Strangely though, everyone I met, be it on the court, field, or green, was kind and encouraging, wanting only to demonstrate how great their particular brand of exercise could be for me. Sport not only broadened my hip flexors, it broadened my mind.
- That a judo gi should never be called pyjamas. Even when saying they're very nice pyjamas.
- To enjoy being part of a team, even though my netball skills probably wouldn't have earned me a place on an under-5s reserve squad.

- That a beginners' game of lawn bowls is one of the world's great levellers. I was beaten just as easily by a grandfather and a pre-schooler.
- That, in spite of what I've always been told, I actually have good hand–eye coordination – as assessed by a Commonwealth silver medal-winning shooter (who I managed not to injure with my efforts).
- How much I value personal space. When kneeling between the legs of a singlet-wearing wrestler, with his happiness resting on my shoulder, I quickly came to terms with my own boundaries.
- That squash balls be fast, and I be slow.
- How easy it is to convince myself that I'm terrible at something, before I've even tried it.
- Not to listen when my head tells me to quit. My body has at least another half a minute / kilometre / pint of sweat to give.
- How insanely useful the skills of throwing and catching are – once I learnt how to do them properly.
- That the end is sometimes the best place to start.

THE END IS SOMETIMES THE BEST PLACE TO START

For most of my life so far, I have been caught in a trap in which so many of us find ourselves, without ever really noticing the chains. I call it "The Waiting Trap" because some things just don't require that much imagination.

I kept waiting. It didn't really matter what I was waiting for: better days, better weather, better luck. Whatever it was that I was pinning my future hopes on gave me an excuse not to move forward until it arrived.

How many of us recognise these statements?

'Once I've lost a few pounds, I'll start meeting new people.'

'I just need to get that promotion, then I can find time to be creative.'

'As soon as he / she / they like me, I will be so much happier.'

Seems reasonable, right? When things are all sorted out, you'll move on. But what if that thing your whole new world depends upon never actually happens?

For me, the trap was usually this one:

'When I feel better, I'll start living my life.'

I really bought in to the fallacy too. I had the clothes that I would wear once my anxiety allowed; there were lists of places I would go when I became the confident version of myself that was surely to come. I even had my eye on the house I would buy, once Paula was able to integrate into a middle-class community.

Did I mention that I waited? I only bring it up again because there was a whole lot of it going on. The month for the new medication to kick in. The 12 weeks for the counselling to really hit home. The month for the new medication to kick back out again. Something was going to change; something was going to start the process. And something did: me.

I stopped waiting.

Now, I'm not pretending it was a purposeful thing. I have no psychic powers and I'm not even particularly intuitive, so to say I had thought the process through to its obvious conclusion would be a big old exaggeration. But what I did know, as soon as I started, was that it was already working. It wasn't a miracle or anything – no shining light showed me the way and there were setbacks pretty much every day – but before too long, I began wearing those clothes and visiting those places I'd been saving for when my mental health improved.

And – surprise, surprise – my mental health started to improve or, at least, I started to recognise that it didn't have to improve for me to be part of my own life.

Don't get me wrong, I was still a mess. I cried almost every morning of the two years that my Glasgow 2014 challenge lasted. I didn't want to face another swimming lesson or plod around a hockey pitch in the snow again. And, most of all, I didn't want to talk to more people and face what they might think of me and my glaring inadequacies, in this alien sporting world. Many times, I fell back into those patterns that I'd been carving out for so long: calling off sick and self-medicating among my favourites. There were panic attacks aplenty, and tantrums that toddlers would envy, but I didn't wait for them to subside before the next effort could begin.

Sometimes, we just have to skip to the end of the process. Start meeting people before losing those few pounds that no one but you notices anyway. Be creative now; the promotion might not allow you that time later. Concentrate on making yourself happier first, and others will naturally warm to you. Or they won't, but at least you'll still be happy. Whatever it is that's holding you back from that ending you're looking towards, let it go.

Give up on waiting, go out there, and just start.

CHAPTER 9

ADVENTURES IN THE LIMELIGHT

By July 2014, life had changed.

Wait, that's not right. By July 2014, life was exactly the same, but I had changed within it. I still went out to work in the morning, but now I didn't need to be walked to my car. I still loved my family, but now I could actually go and visit them. I was still Paula, but now I was just more myself. Or more the person that I always thought I could be.

It's a lovely picture I'm putting together here, right? A picture of a woman so destroyed by anxiety that she could no longer cope with the basic functions of the world, suddenly freed from its tyranny, with nothing standing in her way.

It's a lie, of course, that picture. Well, to be a bit kinder, it's more impressionistic than perhaps it first looks. I've said it before, I know, but I just want to be very clear: running around a bit, and learning to how to do a headstand did not cure my anxiety. I didn't throw a ball and suddenly realise I no longer cared what other people thought of me, or jump so high that I could no longer feel down.

What sport and adventure did for me was much more profound than all that: they taught me to trust myself. They showed me that no matter how difficult I find life, no matter how little I understand it, or how scary it seems, I can rely on myself to cope. Maybe not beautifully or calmly, maybe not always well, but whatever I'm thrown, I know I can handle it – because I'm a goddamn adventurer.

Every day for the two years of my Glasgow 2014 challenge, I had to push myself to tackle something new: a different sport, an unknown playing field, a burly Olympian. Each time, I learnt that I was capable. Not fantastic, not the best, just capable. Even when I was rubbish at the actual activity – and, believe me, it happened a lot – and when people laughed (mostly good-naturedly) at how poorly I performed, I just kept trying. It didn't kill me that I wasn't the best bowler. No one died when I missed the squash ball. The world didn't end when I came last in every race.

Okay, so I never really imagined that society would crumble if I was seen to fail at the long jump, but the exaggeration is not so far away from the truth of social anxiety. Bit by bit, the condition had chipped away at reality until I had absolutely no idea what was frightening and what wasn't. Every fear was just as real as the next, whether that was sharing a meal with a friend, or sharing a park bench with a grizzly bear – I would run screaming from both. Facing things that I had no business being able to face showed me that, no matter what anxiety tells me, or how it makes my body respond, I don't have to believe it. I can just go out and find out the truth for myself instead.

When folk – typically folk who don't know me or my situation – scoff at how I've challenged myself and suggest that I can't really have suffered anxiety at all, I try not to be offended and instead remind myself that it's probably more of a compliment than anything, even if it isn't intended that way. Perhaps now I don't seem anxious, whatever anxious seems like. Perhaps I look a bit more like one of those people who seems to just breeze through things, no matter the storm around them. Maybe I even am one of those people. But it has taken blood, sweat, and more bloody sweat to reach this place and I'd love nothing more than for everyone else to join me here. And, you know, some people actually have.

The first message of encouragement that Paula Must Try Harder received from a stranger truly amazed me.* And the second. And the hundredth. Like I said, I started off on a very selfish journey, to find a way out of my own craziness, and didn't really expect much support, let alone think I might ever be able to support others. Stupidly though, I hadn't factored in the Glasgow 2014 effect. At that time, you could have manufactured dentures and slapped the Commonwealth Games logo across them, and thousands would have bitten your hand off for a set.

Equally though – and never underestimate this strength – I was appallingly bad at sport. This instantly made me an underdog. No one is threatened by an underdog; they find it inspiring or pathetic, but they never want to put it down. Women who had been embarrassed to go back to their hockey team or jogging club, because they didn't know if they still had the skills, could come along with me, since I never had the skills in the first place. Without trying, I was making it alright to be bad at sport – and I was good with that.

Early on, a Glasgow bowling club reached out to invite me to try my fifth sport at their next open day, at which my friend Gav, and I spent several happy hours. Suddenly, I was the kind of person who could be invited to places and, weirder still, I was the kind of person who could accept invitations without wondering instantly how I was going to get out of actually going along.

Soon the media heard of my challenge and decided I might be worth talking about. Or they had run out of other inventive ways to remind readers that, in case they hadn't noticed, the Games were coming to town and they should probably be reading all about them. What they reminded me, however, was that I had an important decision to make. Was I really fit to talk to journalists and broadcasters – to the

* The message itself was a simple note; not of thanks or anything, just of acknowledgement that I was making it acceptable to talk about anxiety. The sender was a fellow sufferer, who hadn't managed to go outside for a while. She was going to try because I had. I replied that I was going to keep trying because she was.

international community, in fact – when only months before I was so tongue-tied talking to a cycling instructor that I spat all down my handlebars?

Of course I wasn't. But that didn't mean I wasn't going to try.

RADIO

You're the best, around. Nothing's gonna ever keep you down ...

The *Karate Kid* theme song blares from the studio speakers, as I perch on the end of the chair I've been ushered towards, and wrestle the headphones over my ears. The cord wraps itself around my arm and I almost knock myself out trying to free it. I'm so far out of my depth, I'm pretty sure the kraken is loitering beneath the mixing desk. This is my first visit to a radio studio and I'm suitably on edge. The presenter, Fred, smiles before introducing to the country someone that could be me, if I just squint my ears a little.

'We're looking ahead to the Commonwealth Games, and after the Olympics we were told there's a sport out there for everyone, but our next guest wasn't too sure; she wasn't a sportswoman, she's Paula McGuire. So she challenged herself to try all 17 sports from the Commonwealth Games list. Let's find out how she's getting on. Good morning, Paula.'

I lean forwards to speak and words come out. They're in a half-decent order and everything. This is unexpected. The entire morning I've been tearing myself apart about agreeing to this interview on BBC Radio Scotland's weekday show. I really don't know what I was thinking. Probably that they would realise, in time, that I'm not broadcastable material and thank me, but no thank me graciously, thereby saving me the embarrassment. They didn't.

Strangely, this seat is quite comfortable now that I've settled in a bit, and it swivels too, which is always great for using up some nervous energy. My knee rattles off the table leg and I stop swivelling, just in time to hear the next question. I'm answering before I know it, just allowing myself to enjoy the conversation for once. I can do this. I've learnt to ride a bike and lifted weights with an Olympian; I can natter into a microphone for a few minutes about how badly it's all been going. Besides, Fred and his co-host, Susan, are only asking questions about me and my life, and, let's face it, if I don't know the answers, I should just leave right now and go for a dementia test. I'm quickly finding my position in the group as idiot savant, and since I normally just think of myself as the idiot, I'm loving the promotion. In my excitement, I've already forgotten to use my polite voice, which I can normally keep up for at least five minutes or so. The room is alive with laughter and chat, and I'm part of it, not loitering on the outskirts, but right at its heart with everyone else. And they seem to be enjoying my contributions, particularly the cycling anecdotes, or any one in which I fall spectacularly. I'm not sure it makes for great radio but we're having a good time. I don't think I've breathed for a while, and I'm giggling like a mad fool, but if I faint from lack of oxygen, at least the audience won't see me go.

'It's really an alternative Commonwealth Games experience.'

'It's Commonwealth Games for people who are talentless.'

'I think you're doing yourself an injustice.'

'You've not seen me doing any sports.'

And now, all at once, it's over. Fred is promising to bring me back on the show for updates, and even offering to take me shooting clays to round off my challenge. I'm ecstatic. I think it went well. In fact, I'm sure it did. I allow myself the tiniest moment of pride.

Heading back downstairs with the producer, an overwhelming surge of weariness hits me. God, I'm tired. I hadn't realised just how much effort talking can take. My sister must be constantly exhausted. I guess all of this morning's pent-up stress has finally found an exit strategy and I've been left without the oomph I need just to make it back to reception. While my legs feel like lead though, my thoughts are still racing ...

I said something stupid, I know I did. They'll never ask me back. I hope no one was listening. Did I offend anyone? I probably did. But I was only talking about sports and my own experience. What if I sounded like a total idiot who thinks she can cure mental health problems with a hockey stick? They knew that's not what I meant, right? Was it clear enough though? I didn't mean to talk so much. I should have thought this through.

Finally, back in the car, I let the anxiety consume me and I cry for a while, worn out and wired.

But now someone else needs this parking space. I should move on.

AFFIRMATIVE ACTION

Yes.

For such a small word, it carries a whole lot of weight, although I wouldn't tell it that to its face. It's also quite addictive, when you're saying it right. I hadn't realised that before, mainly because I never really said it and, if I accidentally did, I never meant it and would take it back as soon as I possibly could.

For things that mattered – family, work, responsibilities – I didn't need spoken affirmations; I was just there, always, no matter what. And for everything else, there were a million other responses that came to mind far quicker than 'yes' ever could, such as, 'no way,' 'not a chance,' and 'absolutely not!'

So the word left my lexicon, without so much as a retirement do. I became closed to possibility, and that was just fine with me. In my scared head, possibility looked exactly like danger: unknown, lurking, ready to kill me or, worse, show me up. I wasn't inviting that sort of nonsense into my life, not even for the chance to actually live it.

Around the time I was juggling sports like a circus decathlete, the yes word started to hang around the periphery once more, edging its way back into my good graces. I wondered if maybe, this time around, I could use it to my advantage. Let's face it, shutting myself down from everything that had caused me anxiety for decades hadn't quite provided the desired results. The fear had only grown ever bigger, and my existence had been squashed into submission. Perhaps there was another way. Perhaps it started with yes.

I tried it out, rolling the syllable around my mouth a few times before spitting it out inadvertently the first time opportunity came a-knocking.

'Would you like to tell your story ...?'

'YES.'

Standing in front of 100 bored teenagers the following week, with 20 minutes left on the clock and only high school flashbacks to keep me company, I was reminded to be a little less eager in future. Before long though, another teacher heard of my talk, then another journalist, and another news programme, and soon a strange new network of avenues and chances lay ahead, all open for me to consider.

That's the thing about yes – it's a gossip. And the more I allowed myself to be talked about, the bigger the world became. Soon, saying yes was normal again; in fact, it was up there with chocolate among my most used words. Don't get me wrong, I'm far from compliant; I can still deploy a "no" with all the force of a thousand Yodas. But, these days, it's not my default, when a promising, interesting, or even just fun experience is on the horizon. I'm not quite running towards it like a Hollywood love interest but I'm certainly open to meeting up for a cuppa.

I can't tell you how much I would have missed out on over the last few years had I continued to hide myself away. It's not a secret or anything, I just don't have a brilliant memory. But there are more than a few joyful, pivotal moments that have crossed my path only because I stepped out onto the path in the first place. Obviously, I'm not saying that I deserved any of this stuff; I'm no more worthy than the next girl – and that next girl probably has some talent to bring to the party. All I'm saying, perhaps inarticulately, is that trusting myself to be up to the challenge, whatever the challenge was, brought me more life than I could ever have imagined and certainly more than I could merit.

Like the time I was on the news for all the right reasons. Or when I had my own national radio slot, *Paula Presents* ..., during the Games. Or that night when a billion people worldwide watched this galoot try not to drop the ball – or the Queen's Baton – at the Glasgow 2014 Opening Ceremony.

CARRYING THE BATON*

Celtic Park is humming with the buzz of 40,000 people, gathering to celebrate the opening of the 2014 Commonwealth Games. From our vantage point, just out of view of the crowd, the stadium looks incredible: all lights and dancing and, yes, giant teacakes.

After two weeks of rehearsals and preparations, costume fittings and choreography, we're finally here, ready to play our part in the biggest show in town. Among our little group are medal-winning athletes, a Gladiator, and coaches who have changed the lives of many. Every one of these 25 people has been hand-picked for their services to sport. I'm very lucky – and bewildered – to be waiting in the wings with these special individuals, and I feel it. My insides are upside down behind my coordinated outfit. I've never performed on the world's stage before, and there's plenty that could go wrong. Each step I'm about to take has been carefully arranged and painstakingly practised so that our path across the field is graceful and disaster-free.

Film stars and TV presenters pass by or stop for photos, and the excitement of the occasion is churning in a big, squealing mess around our backstage area. Then the call goes up through our earpieces and we're off, jostling forwards to take our starting positions on the pitch as the music I hum, even in my sleep, fills the air. The melody is haunting, and the mood quietens, and as we start to move, all I can hear are the instructions in my ear to keep smiling.

The lights follow our progress as the baton passes between us in sequence, each of us in turn moving it towards its ultimate goal. Always travelling, never paused, just like we've performed it all week long. Only, this time, there are more than just the stage-hands and security staff watching.

In a moment that we all knew would be spectacular, Ashley, one of the youngest among us, is hoisted aloft, her smile dazzling, as we circle around. If there's an image that sums up the experience for our team, it's most definitely this one. As she's lowered delicately back to ground, she hands on the baton. For a moment it is in my hands, and I grip the elm wood handle tightly. Before now, we've been using a stunt double, and this real baton is jarringly heavier than the polystyrene stand-in. We've been reminded that our hands will be in shot and any nail polish should be chip-free, since the cameras will surely pick up our disgrace. I don't have the nails for polishing anyway, but I'm slightly concerned that the world might be currently seeing a close-up of my hairy thumbs.

Passing on the baton and my duty, I fall into step with the rest of the pack. We're picking up speed now, trotting towards the last of our relay, Sir Chris Hoy, who will deliver the baton to the Queen, in the royal box above. It's almost over, this wonderful few weeks, and I look around at the crowd and the stage and the friends I've made, and I store it all away.

I'm scared as hell but I'm here, and that's enough for me.

THE LOST AND FOUND

What happens when you lose everything that you've ever known about yourself?

Not in a Marty McFly, disappearing from the photo album, kind of way. But when the rock that you've built your entire personality around suddenly crumbles, what's left? I know how stupid it must sound, but I felt completely lost when I first realised that I could no longer depend on anxiety to be my foundation. I've said it before but even repetition adds to my word count: anxiety was all I knew of my own personality for the longest time. Frightened, nervous, timid – every adjective in my armoury hung around that same theme. So when they began, gradually, to abandon me, I couldn't quite find solid ground. Once stripped of that instant reaction of fear, I wasn't sure what I felt about anything.

Do I like parties? I don't know. Tigers are kinda cute but I'm not sure I'd cuddle one. How do I really feel about wind turbines?

Joking aside, this bright new world of rediscovery was disconcerting – and not just for me. Friends who had been in my life since childhood were witnessing a real difference in my outlook – in the person they thought they knew – and at times, they didn't know how to respond. I'm not ashamed to say I was devastated by their reactions. Here I was, dealing with some of my most difficult battles, fighting to steal myself back from mental illness, and some of the people I had always been there for, who I thought were there for me, just disappeared. Now that I no longer just sat in a corner, reliable and steadfast, and without a life of my own, those friends had no time to lend me the support I had so often given freely to them.

Or that's how I saw it at first.

In retrospect, I can see that I had changed, more than a little. While that change was so positive for me, it's not really my place to say how it affected those I loved. Maybe those friends just didn't know how to relate to me any more. Maybe they didn't actually like the person I was becoming. Maybe I just talked too bloody much now. Whatever their reasons were, that's exactly what they were – *their* reasons. Not mine to second guess or rail against. But I won't deny it took me a good few sobbing sessions to recognise that.

Don't cry for me though, bambina. My social circle has turned into a full globe since I made the leap into a three-dimensional reality, but for a long enough time, I worried that I was only making my situation worse. What if anxiety was the only thing keeping me a decent person? Maybe I was utterly vile underneath, just waiting for the courage to wreak havoc. Oh, how Gerry laughed, every single day for over a year, when I checked if I had become a monster. Fine, the laughing stopped after the first week or so, but he still seemed vaguely amused by the concept long afterwards. The question was genuine though. Anxiety had me so caught in its trap that I was terrified to escape, in case the cage wasn't only keeping me safe from the world; in case it was keeping the world safe from me too.

Over everything else though, my biggest concern had to be my marriage. Gerry had been by my side for every second of challenge and triumph but, as I constantly reminded him, he was now married to a completely different Paula than the one he'd taken for toast on that first date, or the one who hadn't been able to enjoy a first dance with him at our wedding. His reply was simple, and still is, every time I push him on the issue.

'You're still the same Paula you always were at home. Now that Paula can just go outside and talk to other people too.'

TEDX

I slip off my shoes and pad over to the red circle at the front of the stage.

'I was always told not to wear my shoes on the carpet.'

The audience laughs and I relax a little. I hadn't planned to say it; I certainly hadn't rehearsed the line. I'm not sure it would have made it past the selection process. TEDx is a slick affair, and I feel like the burst couch of the day. I've brushed my hair and everything, but still, I'm standing in my stockinged feet, in front of 600 people, and already I'm saying words that weren't part of the show plan.

Every other element of the event is carefully considered and managed; from the colour-coded speakers' badge around my neck to the volunteer I've been allocated for support. He's lovely, so we had a nice chat. Then I suggested he might as well go and enjoy the other talks, since I'd been fetching my own sandwiches for a number of years and was pretty sure I wouldn't start needing someone else to do it today.

My eyes rest momentarily on the floor monitor screen, counting down the time I have left to speak. The organisers allotted me six minutes, which began the instant I opened my mouth so I've already used up 20 seconds on a joke that wasn't even part of my speech. I'm pretty sure Judy Murray used all of her time effectively earlier this afternoon. Her shoes probably stayed on throughout too. That's why she's the professional.

I am definitely a rank amateur. Amateur because this is my first proper speaking gig outside of schools and charities; rank because I'm currently standing in front of a far-too-big projection of my bare arse. It seemed like a wonderful idea, likening my naked rear-end to the horrors of social anxiety, and I reckon I'm putting the point across, but I hadn't quite thought through the part where I stand for a full minute beneath my own massive crack.

'So what does my backside have to do with anxiety? Actually, more than you think.'

The theatre looks scarily impressive from this angle, I try but fail not to notice. I've been in the Tramway before, hiding somewhere in the middle rows at a Shakespeare performance in high school, terrified that audience participation might break out and I could be caught in the crossfire. Now I'm up front, hoping for any audience participation that isn't booing. So far, they seem kind; chuckling in the right places and not appearing to mind that I can't stop moving.

That's the great thing about anxiety talks – everyone expects you to be anxious while giving them. And I am not letting them down. A man in the front row catches my eye. He smiles. It's all the reassurance I need. Maybe he knows what I'm coping with; maybe he just feels a little sorry for me. Either way, that fleeting connection with another human being, with someone that I would never otherwise have met, reminds me why I'm up here.

I smile back and, in the warmth of the shared moment, completely forget my next line. I've practised this talk so many times I almost went hoarse. I've recited it to the sea on a trip to Troon, my favourite park has heard it from each swing within its grounds, and now, when it matters, I cannot remember how the next bit goes. Is it the part about blinking too much? No, I'm sure that comes later. Crap! It's gone, it's completely gone. I don't know how long I've been floundering. I think just a second or two, since no one has burst on stage yet to end all our suffering.

Then I remember. It doesn't matter what happens, only how I respond to it. It's not important that I dropped the ball, only that I pick it back up. I can freeze and panic, or scurry away, or I can just keep going.

'So I became Paula Must Try Harder – the most lacklustre superhero name ever. I became the girl who tried everything, the everyday adventurer.'

It's not quite the next line of the script. I've missed something out, but no one else knows that, and the narrative seems to be hanging together without it anyway. I bounce on my heels a little, geeing myself up, not allowing my head to become stuck in its old, destructive patterns. I'll beat myself up a little later, it's a certainty, but that's a battle for another time. Right now, all I have to do is talk. 'Be afraid, be very afraid, because it's good for you!'

The clock is nearing its final countdown and I'm back on track with my message for the day: living it as well as speaking it. I am afraid. I'm afraid that I haven't seen the last of that mental block or that, in 53 seconds, when I'm due to leave the stage, it will be to silence; only the sound of me shoving my retreating feet into my abandoned pumps echoing around the hall. Somehow, the image makes me laugh and I'm struck by the utter absurdity of the situation.

Me, Paula McGuire, shoeless and shaking, explaining social anxiety to a theatre full of strangers, with the TEDx logo at my back. I deliver the closing lines, safe in the knowledge that the world has gone mad, and I'm finally one among many.

'Thank you.' I curtsy – God only knows why – and it's done.

THINGS I LEARNT FROM THE LIMELIGHT

- That imagining people in the audience naked – as delightful as it sounds – only serves to make you feel a bit sick and distract you from your original point. Unless your original point is that no one looks good in the buff.
- To always just be myself – as Disney princess as that sounds. Nothing undercuts a message more than it sounding like it came from a book on authenticity. People respond to people. So if I'm nervous, I admit it; on stage, on air, or just in conversation. That way, folk know what to expect, and my nerves aren't allowed to get in the way.

- That a trip to the local supermarket, even after you've just had tea with Prince Imran of Malaysia, will always bring you back down to reality.
- How to answer the same question, asked by three enthusiastic children one after the other, in three completely different ways.
- When something goes well, it's great. When something goes badly, it's a great story.
- That all people, no matter how fresh-faced they look on screen, have bad days and tired eyes.
- To give my own opinions equal weighting to everyone else's. Just because they speak with more authority than my inner voice will ever have, doesn't mean they know what they're talking about. A pound of feathers – no matter how soft – holds just as much weight.
- The benefits of having a theme tune. Playing Joe Esposito's 'You're the Best Around' at top volume upgrades any grey morning to a vibrant shade of pink. My neighbours must think I have an obsession with Ralph Macchio.* I don't think I'll ever put them right.
- That when you want to shut someone up quickly, turn on a microphone. Nothing quite sucks the chat out of a room like a recording device.
- To turn barriers into climbing frames.

* The original Karate Kid, whose theme tune I have commandeered as my own. If he wants it back, he can have it though. I've seen how that guy fights.

TURNING BARRIERS INTO CLIMBING FRAMES

I'm so thankful for my anxiety.

Rest assured, I have not lost my mind in that last page turn. Everything that has gone before is still true, and all the difficult days to come will still come. But, I repeat, I'm so, so thankful for my anxiety. I added an extra "so" but I'm sure you'll forgive the oversight.

I don't relish its effects on my blood pressure, or enjoy the digestive discomfort any more than I ever have, but those 30 years of fear have given me so much more than just a heightened sense of dread and the beginnings of an ulcer. They've given me a barrier and showed me how strong I can be by finding my way over it.

I promise, I haven't gone all inspirational quote on you. You can make whatever the hell you like with those lemons life has given you. But, for me, anxiety has become a bona fide blessing. Even writing those early chapters, with tears streaking my plump cheeks (cake helps me work), I felt drained and saddened, but, now more than anything, I feel alive. I haven't walked away from anxiety; you don't just sneeze it out and bin the tissue. No, it's better than all that. It's still with me, but now I know its game. Anxiety is a bitch, but it's my bitch.

Since as far back as I can remember, I was so ashamed of my nerves; I tried so hard to hide them, making them even more obvious to see. Anxiety embarrassed me, it disabled me, and, worse, it cut me off from the one thing in which I would finally find solace: other people. I hated anxiety. It was the source of all my problems and would, I was sure, be my undoing. I had to get rid of it so that I could have the life I wanted. NOPE.

The life I wanted was indeed on the other side of anxiety, but I didn't need to wait for transport to get over there, what I needed was to make my own way. The lessons were all in the hike, in the struggle, and I'm a much tougher soul for having learnt them. Anxiety is the reason I'm sitting here today. It's the reason that I can talk to young people about good mental health from a position of experience – of both sides. It's the reason I can now connect with others in a way that I never thought would be possible for me.

Anxiety put up a huge wall around me, and I'm just a little bit proud of the person I've become by climbing over it. We all – every confident, well rounded, self-assured one of us – come up against crap in this world. Forging our own route over that crap can be sheer hell, but it can also show us exactly where we should be.

For 30 years, I lived with anxiety; now anxiety has to live with me.

CHAPTER 10

ADVENTURES IN FLIGHT

In the weeks following the Commonwealth Games, I was scared.

By rights, I'm sure, I should have been feeling relieved; maybe even a little cheerful. I had set myself a challenge and succeeded, not only in trying the 17 sports before my self-imposed deadline, but also in finding a way back into the world. And, of course, I was feeling those things too, deep down, in those parts of our anatomy saved for secrets and lonely nights. Mostly though, I was worried for my future: a future I had never really considered having, so hadn't exactly planned for extensively.

My horizons had suddenly broadened so much they took up my whole field of view. But I couldn't allow myself to just run towards them, bright skies or not, because I wasn't sure if what I was looking at was real, or just a mirage conjured up by the excitement of my new outlook. What if the only thing saving me from anxiety's clutches was my Glasgow 2014 challenge? And now that it was done, what if I just reverted back?

After all the hubbub of the previous few years, keeping me busy and pushed to my limits, the quiet of the aftermath was disconcerting. I no longer recognised normal life, so how was I meant to return to it? Did I even want to return? The world in my head was different and I wasn't sure I knew how to go back to the one outside of it. My recovery felt fragile, unfamiliar. I hadn't expected to ever reach this point; there was never a schedule for this kind of improvement, so I wasn't sure if I was on it or not. I hadn't made a list as I'd gone along of the things that had helped most, or those that had caused me to falter. Maybe wrestling strangers on a floor mat was the cure and I'd just breezed through the experience without saving the ingredients for times still to come. How was I to know? The experiment hadn't been carried out under laboratory conditions; I had no way of recreating the results.

But perhaps they were permanent. Perhaps this new-found mindset might just be mine to keep. I had to test it, just to be sure. So I stopped. For a few weeks, I lived the way I always had – only without the shackles. And I was horrifically, interminably bored. How had I managed to survive like this for so long? Don't get me wrong, I quite enjoyed the laziness of it all; I've never understood folk who stop at just 40 winks. For the most part though, I was uninspired. I don't doubt that much of my ennui was a front for the build-up of nervous energy and concern that had nowhere to go. Flutters of fear still punctuated even my most uneventful days, but overall, I felt fine – just not quite as alive as before.

Adventure, it seemed, hadn't just been tempering the anxiety to lift me onto a level playing field. It had been building me a playing field all of my own. Not a temporary one, but one on which I could really live my life. If all it would take for me to stay healthy and engaged was to continue trying new things and confronting my fears, then it was a price worth paying.

Then it was decided. I would just keep going. Paula Must Try Harder – and she would.

The next adventure found me before I had the time to go out and look for it. I don't know if you know this, but children are full of ideas. Not having been one, even when I was one, I hadn't realised quite how accidentally insightful kids were, until I was invited to speak in schools more and more about my sporting efforts. Afterwards, as their hands shot up to ask the most wonderfully varied questions, there would be stories – lots of stories – about their own adventures and, more often, about the adventures they had planned for when they grew up. They would be farmers and actors and astronauts and racing drivers. They would be whatever they wanted to be. Their voices were sure and excited. There was no doubt. That's when I realised, standing in front of a gym hall full of youngsters, that I'd always known what I wanted to be too. In fact, most of the adults in my life had known what they wanted to be when they left school, but barely any of us had actually followed through with the ambition – including me.

Since the first time I read a book and realised that it was actually someone's job to conjure such eloquent magic, I wanted to be a writer. As I wrapped myself in the safari jacket of those adventure-filled pages, there was nothing I wanted more than to share the joy of words with others the way Roald Dahl and C.S. Lewis so kindly did with me. I was the kid who kept pens in her ponytails, who asked for a typewriter for Christmas, who wrote poetry while friends rode scooters.

Throughout my accounting degree and my stint as a support worker, even during the bus driver training and post-sorting, I never stopped dreaming about writing. So, when did I stop aiming for it? Maybe aged eight, when I was (mis)informed that only rich people write books. Or at 12, when I realised that not trying definitely meant not failing. It might even have lasted until my twenties, when life finally took hold and hopes were confined to the past. Whenever it was, I let it happen and for that, childhood, I'm sorry.

What I really didn't want, however, was for the next generation of bright young minds to let the world convince them that they couldn't work their way towards their goals, just because of where they come from or their overwhelming pet allergies. I'm sure lots of vets take antihistamines.

Thus began the next challenge, and my attempt to show that, if an unqualified fool from downtown nowhere can fly a plane or fight a fire, there's no reason for anyone to ever trade down on their dreams.

THE DREAM JOBS CHALLENGE

[From the blog – August 2014]

The challenge:

With a little help from the internet – and a whole host of surveys with actual research behind them – I've collated a list of the top jobs that kids want for their grown-up selves. You know, before they start worrying about stability, practicality and the availability of decent cheese in the nearest supermarket. And over the next year or so, I'm going to try every single daunting one of them, starting with my own. I'll be attempting to teach, fly, and farm, to design the next Tetris, and set the Nürburgring alight (only figuratively, I hope). And yes, astronaut is on the list, so expect some letters, NASA.

It might be stupid, it's probably a tad ambitious, and it's definitely going to be tough as old boots with a black belt, but I'm going to try anyway, because aspirations are the life-blood of childhood, and we shouldn't let doubt, time, or poor advice tear them so readily asunder.

The list:

Well, here it is, my career path for the next 12 months, all 16 wayward strands of it. Wish me luck, laugh at my progress, or enjoy my failings, but whatever you do, don't send your cat for a check-up this winter.

Writer

Farmer

Teacher

Athlete

Police Officer Firefighter Paramedic

Pilot

Vet

Singer / musician

Actor

Astronaut

Racing driver

Scientist

Computer game designer

Adventurer

It wouldn't be a challenge if it looked easy.

Pilot

The tarmac disappears. We're not only in the air, we're barrelling through it. And it feels incredible.

Andy's voice crackles through my headphones.

'How are you feeling, Paula?'

I should say something eloquent, capture the moment of lifting away from life below in clever, rousing words.

'Woooooooooooo!'

It's all I have, and I stand by it. I raise two thumbs as well though, in case Andy didn't quite catch my meaning from his position behind me in the Extra EA-300 aircraft. As a member of The Blades aerobatic display team and an ex-Red Arrow, he's probably not slow on the uptake though, I imagine.

It's noisy as hell, with the roar of the engine and the blood pounding in my ears, and I have to press hard against the sides of the headset to make out Andy's commentary. Until I hear his comment that there's a volume control.

'Look over to your left.'

I do as I'm told, since I'm pretty much here on luck and goodwill, and I'm not sure how long luck will keep me airborne without Andy's goodwill. Almost within touching distance, it seems, is another identical plane: Andy's teammate, flying in formation, mirroring our movement as we rip across the sky. Our little flock feels untouchable, beyond anything that the universe can throw at us, and I can just look on in childlike wonderment with eyes so wide they're contemplating a diet.

Andy checks if I'm ready for us to fly a loop and it takes me all my willpower not to just ask him to marry me. In an instant, we're climbing, feeling every thrust of the G force as we pull into the curve, my head driven backwards, giddy and giggling, against the neck rest. Everything has changed; perspective means nothing when you're looking at the world from all the wrong angles. As quickly as we're in, we're back out again, straightening up, then into another. Barrel rolls that change the axis of rotation, moving around the other plane like skaters in perfect sync. Breathtaking trickery that I just can't fathom, but am so glad that Andy can.

'Do you want to take over for the next loop?'

Is there any other answer to that question than the one that blurts from my mouth? 'Of course!'

I'm so glad he told me about the volume switch because I reckon I'll really need to be listening to this next bit. Andy straightens us up then talks me through what I'm about to do, before giving me a countdown, and we're off. As quickly as that. Up and over, my stomach performing its own spins with equal and opposite might. My stupid big grin is so genuine it has provenance, and I'm laughing with all my bones.

I fly another, and another, before Andy takes back control for more swirls and stalls. We're in a bubble, tipping towards land, end over end; smoke trails behind. No, in front. Hell, I'm no longer sure.

This, right here, is living. It's not just the flying; it's the sense of taking back a freedom that anxiety has always tried to steal away. The girl who could not face her own doorstep, who struggled with life at its very foundations is, at last, above it all.

AND THE REST ...

Writer: Since it would have been slightly hypocritical to encourage others to go after their dream jobs without ever having gone after mine, it was only fair that I start here. 94 hours, 10 gallons of tea, and enough Victoria sponge to absorb the Atlantic, and I'd written a book – albeit a terrible one – and self-published my quick-lit novel for no one to buy, ever. I'd proved the point though, that my excuse of never having the time was as bogus as my plot-line.

Farmer: Old MacDonald had nothing on this city slicker, as I pulled on my wellies and chanced my arm as a farm-hand. From the delight of weighing piglets, to the trauma of mucking out the sheep pens, every task brought with it a brand-new smell to take back to town. Sharing the experience with the packed bus home was a particular pleasure.

Police Officer: I'm as surprised as you are that I managed to survive the security checks, and was invited to visit the police college for a few days of training. Drill practice, vehicle searches and drug checks, all in a uniform that weighed more than my conscience. But the part I enjoyed most was the corridor interaction. 'Good morning, Ma'am,' with a nod; a door held open and a hat raised. I could get used to that kind of treatment. Baton training came a close second.

Singer: I can't hold a tune with a clamp so Scottish Opera weren't quite holding a part open for me after our time together. I did manage to put across an entire aria from *The Marriage of Figaro* to their soprano singing coach, but I'm pretty sure she wanted to pass it back halfway through. A choir recital and performance session later and I was jubilant; off-key, but jubilant.

Astronaut: One of my happiest moments to date was spent spinning gleefully on one of only a handful of long-arm centrifuge machines in the world, used to test the physical reactions of astronauts and fighter pilots to high G forces. Before starting to pass out, at around 3.6 G, I must have looked like the luckiest lady on the planet – and beyond. One of my proudest moments was when I found out that my emails had been bandied about most of NASA before they determined I was too much of a pest to ignore, and introduced me to the relevant people.

Scientist: As someone for whom science class was just an hour of avoiding being set on fire with a Bunsen burner, I wasn't quite sure how to go about this one, but Glasgow Science Centre came to my rescue with a Paula Must Try Science day of events: chromatography, a lichen identification field trip, and even a part to play in the educational production of Blood, Bile and Body Bits. (I was the flatulence mixer.)

Athlete: While I felt that I already had this one covered (did I mention that I tried 17 sports?), it seemed like a cheat to skip it, so instead of another egg-and-spoon lesson, I spent a day training like an athlete at the Institute of Sport, with a Scottish wheelchair racer, Meggan. After a few hours of professional coaching, nutrition, psychology, and physio inputs, I was all the sportsperson I was ever going to be. They didn't ask me back.

Racing driver: Both rallies in which I competed were experiences all to themselves: 90 miles per hour along winding forest tracks, or screeching our way around a military range. As co-driver, it was my job to read the runes of the course – otherwise known as the pace-notes – and plot safe passage for our car and its occupants to the end of each stage. Fortunately, on both occasions, the drivers were excellent – earning us places on the podium – since my navigation skills were so lacking that I got us lost twice on the way to the start line.

Firefighter: Time spent learning how to be fire-retardant is time well spent, in my book. At the Scottish Fire and Rescue Service's training centre, I was shown the ropes of this incredible profession. Unfortunately, the ropes were on fire. And they weren't ropes. They were walls and roofs, and they were burning all around us. I soon found out that I'm a dab hand with a hose and a controlled blaze and, while I didn't end my time as a firefighter with a medal for bravery, I did still have my eyebrows. Small wins.

Vet: Don't worry, no animals were injured in the making of this challenge. While I'm an incredibly dedicated person, it takes almost a decade of study, and a better knowledge of what end to put the thermometer in than I'll ever have, to become a vet. The alternative was to leave it to the skilled professionals, and just go along to help them out at a national wildlife centre. That way, the injured animals were in safe hands, and mine were free to feed baby hedgehogs.

Paramedic: I've never felt so lucky to be sitting in the back of an emergency vehicle, sirens blaring, as we raced across city centre traffic. In my Ambulance Service helmet and hi-vis jacket, I looked the part: if the part was a child pretending to be a paramedic. I could only look on as the real ambulance crew performed tests and administered medication, and gave care well beyond their job description, but if holding an elderly man's hand all the way back to the hospital was the least I could do that day, it was still the most powerful.

Teacher: If I had a hat, I'd raise it to anyone who chooses to educate other people's kids for a living: I don't do headwear, but I have impeccable manners. One day of teaching a class of five-year-olds, and I was hopscotching my way to exhaustion. And I was only entrusted with the fun bits of the lessons: ticking correct answers and coordinating story-time. God knows how I would have coped with long division.

Computer game designer: I know as much about computer games as the Mario brothers know about u-bends, so learning how they're developed, from concept to console, was a fair way from my usual game-play. But after sessions in coding and 3D artistry, and a Virtual Reality master-class with some industry experts, even this thoroughly old-fashioned Millie had picked up a thing or two about bits and PCs.

Actor: Bats have always been in and around my belfry, so it wasn't much of a theatrical stretch for me to play a vampire in an independent supernatural series. Sipping a goblet of blood that tasted a heck of a lot like blackcurrant squash, while miming conversation with a friendly werewolf, was just about all the dramatic range I could muster. The make-up artists were impressed though, since I already resemble a member of the undead.

Adventurer: I'll admit, I thought I might just sneak past this one wearing my monogrammed crampons, but sometimes you just have to throw in that little bit more of yourself …

BUNGEE-JUMPING

'Who wants to go first?'

My hand shoots up so quickly, I almost tumble over the railings. Looking around the assembled group, it seems I needn't have been quite so energetic since I don't have any competition for front of the queue. I'm always the same now when it comes to volunteering; my voice finds itself before I have the chance to properly hide it. But, standing on the metal gantry, suspended from the underside of Garry Bridge, peering down through the grille to the water below, I'm pretty sure the last thing I need is more time to consider my decision.

Nine of us follow the instructor along the walkway to our jumping point, ensuring pockets are emptied and shoelaces are tightly tied along the way. Most of the gathered group are novices and, while the rest have come in twos or threes, I'm on my own up here. Gerry is waiting by the foot of the bridge to capture the moment, or call the ambulance. Either way, I'm glad he's nearby.

Nervous chatter erupts every few minutes but I'm not quite relaxed enough to join in. The funny thing is, I'm not so bothered about falling from a height, great or otherwise. I'm pretty sure the rig is safe and, if you can't trust big elastic bands, what can you trust? I'm mostly just anxious about what the others are thinking of my eagerness to lead the charge. They're probably already saying I'm a show-off, or that I'm trying too hard. Maybe I am. I'm not sure why I care, but I do. I'm just about to step off a 40-metre platform and the only thing worrying me is what a few folk, that I'll never meet again, will think of me.

Oh, and the water. My relationship with the wet stuff has always been more strained than a Christmas Day waistband, and even though I've been making headway with my swimming lessons, I'm still not completely comfortable, even around such calm waterways. Not so long ago, an accidental stroll onto a bridge at night ended in me being carried back, sobbing like a fallen child. Now I'm planning to jump from one. It doesn't seem like the best idea, but here we are anyway.

I force myself to look down again, as the instructor calls me forward to attach the ankle cuffs that will save me from what's below. We've already been weighed twice, just in case we've managed to sneak in some extra calories during the short trip from reception to the riverside, and I'm trying not to feel judged by the number of kilos scrawled on the back of my hand. Apparently, I'm a 51Y, meaning I'll be attached to the yellow cord for my jump. Bungee is not for the colour blind.

Everyone is watching as I waddle, penguin-style, to the end of the narrow gangplank. I know it's the equipment's performance they're interested in, rather than my own, but I still wish I could just do this without an audience. Situations like this always turn up the social anxiety and, even though I've lived with it for so long, it still manages to surprise me at times.

My toes are over the edge, tickling the nothingness beyond, and my face is throwing smiles to the photographer that my emotions can't match. I just want to go now, to be out of sight-lines for just a minute or two, even if it is hurtling towards the riverbed. 'Three, two, one,' and my prayers are answered.

I jump. Well, more just fall, but I'm too busy plummeting to care.

Dropping, spinning, trusting my mass to the air that's hissing past my ears; hopeful that any moment, any moment now ... And suddenly that yellow cord bites back, reaching full extension, and at last, taking the strain. I follow it upwards – it's persuasive but not nearly as violent as I expected. The bounce is forceful but not aggressively so. I've felt more yank at a friendly thanksgiving. Instead it allows me a few moments to just enjoy the sensation of springing and the strange, inverted view of the countryside: its autumnal colours spectacular, even from this angle.

I'm laughing, maybe a little hysterically, as the winch line finds me, and I hook myself to its promise of safety overhead. Somehow, I'm no longer really thinking about the people who wait there, although their enthusiastic cheers are hailing me ever upwards. No matter how much weight my anxiety attributes to the opinions of others, I've just shown myself, once more, that the only opinion that can change things for me is my own – all 51Y of it.

EVERYDAY ADVENTURES

Just the other day, while brushing my teeth, I realised how much more engaged in life I've become. A strange place to contemplate my progress, I'll admit, but it wasn't so much the activity, as my reaction to it, that highlighted the change.

I dropped my toothbrush in the sink.

'Oooh.'

That's the noise I made, not the noise it made. Either way, it wasn't quite the expected response. Normally, I would have let the incident pass without remark. Toothbrushes fall. As long as my teeth don't go with them, I'm usually happy to just let the matter go. This time though, my larynx decided to get involved.

'Oooh.'

The sound was out of my face before I could shut it. It meant nothing, just a momentary utterance. But it made me realise how often such little expressions of interest in the world escape my mouth these days. I giggle when I fall over in public, I gasp aloud when a book surprises me. I'm no longer watching every word, in case I say the wrong thing, so sometimes other sounds bubble to the surface too.

And it's not just noises either. I reach up to touch trees overhead, I stop to stare at the antics of crows, I walk along the cracks in pavements, following them wherever they lead. Sure, passers-by sometimes look on as though I'm crazy, but it's the least crazy I've ever been.

Nowadays, I don't need to rein myself in; I can trust myself off the leash. While ploughing through my Dream Jobs challenge, adventure developed not only into my personal therapy, but also into my link with the world. By taking on other people's occupations and connecting with them in their domain, I wasn't just living my own life, I was, for a little while, trying to live theirs too. I wore their uniforms and learnt their language; quite literally walking in their shoes at times. And I recognised how similar we all are – just bumbling through as best we can, dealing with things in our own ways. As I tried on each different living, I appreciated life just a little more. The experiences changed how I interact with others, and finally made me believe that I do have the ability to just be part of the gang – or not be part of it. (Not seems to suit me better.)

That doesn't mean I don't enjoy being among people now. I hope I've put across just how debilitating the social element of my anxiety really was, and how joyful it is for me just to be a functioning part of the populace at last. Adventure was my gateway into society, and into a community all of my own. The wonderful thing now is that I don't feel the need to impress that community, or only play within its boundaries. That gate swings both ways.

When each job on the list had been thoroughly ticked off, I was already branching out, trying new activities that didn't need categorising to be worthwhile. Life and adventure had merged into one, and they no longer needed separating. You see, when even the most basic human task is new to you, because you've never had the mental wherewithal to face it, you can find adventure in absolutely anything. Just eating in a restaurant with friends, or running through the park on my own was a fresh new exploit, and I could gain just as much from the fear on my doorstep as from following it anywhere else.

This next challenge would be all about adding a little extra to the ordinary. My Everyday Adventures: embracing all that life has to offer, from the banal to the bizarre, with a little bit of the barmy in between.

WING-WALKING

The floor beneath me pitches to the right and I'm reminded that the floor beneath me is actually the roof of a small aircraft. Okay, I never really forgot, but it wouldn't be as difficult as it sounds. There's just something so very peaceful about this whole crazy situation.

I'm 5,000 feet or so above ground, perched on what I can only describe as a deckchair with a good PR team, and, for once, I'm not questioning my life choices. It seems as though all I needed was to be carried skyward on the back of a bright yellow biplane to realise that I'm doing alright.

Basically, I'm a hood ornament in leggings, but just sitting up here, with nothing else to do but enjoy the ride is cathartic ...

'Wheeeeeeeeeeeeeeeeeeeeeeeeeee.'

Cathartic, with moments of real elation thrown in. Below me, actually inside the plane, the pilot, Mike, is dipping us towards the lush Yorkshire fields, almost close enough to graze the grass, then soaring straight back up towards the kind of clouds I've only ever seen in kids' paintings. England has really turned the weather on for my visit and, although I'm here on my own, after a five-hour drive, and just before a five-hour return journey, I'm feeling right at home.

I raise my hands high in the air, enjoying how the wind tugs them backwards, but making sure that at no point do my thumbs point down, since this is Mike's signal to end the flight. Unless a pterosaur appears on the horizon, my thumbs are staying firmly upright.

I'm not worried, I'm not anxious, I'm not even bothered that the safety specs are planting oil rings around my eyes for the waiting crowd of strangers to enjoy. I'm just alive.

Another drop landwards, a quick bank left, and we're gliding higher once more, rolling like a coaster off its tracks. I've been in some aeroplanes in my time, as a kid on special family holidays, or taking trips as a teenager. I've even jumped out of one. But this isn't anything like travelling. No roof above to separate me from the skies; no window to peer through longingly. Just me, my earplugs, and the heavens. What more could I possibly want?

This is flight – or, as a human, as close as I'll ever come to it – and I'm not letting it pass me by without some old-fashioned celebration. Pushed back into the rig, the force of the world my safety net, I throw shapes like a 90s raver. I'm probably just as high.

A final sudden swoop that makes my heart leap like a frightened cat, and we come in to land: a perfect kiss against the ground.

THINGS I LEARNT FROM FLIGHT

- That someone tucking a sick-bag into your pocket is the best incentive ever not to throw up. Tucking the unused sick-bag back into their pocket afterwards is the reward.
- The difference between an anxious stomach flip, and an actual stomach flip. The latter is much more fun.
- That the difference between fear and excitement is only in how we respond to it. And in the pronunciation.
- How to find peace, even while sitting on top of a Boeing Stearman, hurtling towards a field. Seriously, it's kind of soothing.
- That all I had to do to be the perfect wife was secure Gerry a spot on the long-arm centrifuge. Apparently, the way to my man's heart is through his ambition to be an astronaut – or through his ribcage.
- How close I've always been to looking like a movie star. Old-time goggles, a seat atop a plane and a little bit of engine smog, and before you can hold up a "BOOM" inter-title, I'm Buster Keaton's double.
- The truth in the saying that it's always sunny above the clouds.
- To get out of my head and into my life.

GETTING OUT OF MY HEAD AND INTO MY LIFE

For such a small person, I have a big head.

Hold up, there's no need to take me down a peg or two; really, there isn't. I am already on the lowest peg, with only laundry beneath me. Truly, I pride myself on not having a boastful bone in my body – and even that's almost a conceit too far. Where my vanity falls short though, my physiology more than steps up – and it drags my huge skull with it. Yep, there's no two ways about it, mainly because once you've gone the first way around my head, you're far too tired to do it again: I'm just a slave to a big old bonce. It's no wonder then that I spent such a long time living inside its confines, since it's such a spacious pad to occupy. What it wasn't, however, was comfortable. If you've ever been in the eye of a panic attack, you'll recognise that your own mind can be a stormy place, without sanctuary, and without an exit hatch. There's no running away once you're caught inside because everywhere you go, it's with you. It is you. You're just lugging it around, bringing your own rain to the parade.

When I found adventure, without really knowing it, I found a way to enjoy the storm, instead of always trying to hide from it. I don't plan to fill pages hereafter describing the benefits of mindfulness; for one thing, I think planning kind of goes against its teachings. But mostly, I don't really know much about it. I stumbled into a kind of mindfulness all of my own, somewhere between home and the top of a biplane, and it just stuck with me. Not routinely, I want to be clear: there are no 10-minute meditations in my daily routine and the only colouring book I own has Rainbow Brite on the cover.

For me, it's just the joy of being present – if I can say that without sounding like a new-age old-timer. Connecting with reality, whether that was at a weightlifting session, or while chasing down a piglet, reminded me that the nonsense going on in my brain was just noise, drowning out what's actually important: like living my actual life. I didn't need to retreat into my cavernous headspace to figure out the answers. I needed to cuddle some damn piglets, or lift a few kilos. As soon as I was fully conscious of what was going on outside, all that stuff inside retreated to the background. It wasn't less rowdy or vocal, just more in perspective.

Turns out, anxiety is a real attention seeker, but as soon as I had other things to attend to, I started to see it for what it really was: a mental health condition, a constant challenge, but not my present. And certainly not my future.

CHAPTER 11

ADVENTURES IN THE NUDE

I'm not big on hatred. In fairness, I'm not big on many things; even stepladders. But constantly burning with resentment, kicking out more heat than light, seems to me like a huge source of wasted energy. I just don't understand it.

For such a long time, without even realising, my morale had been spiralling downwards. Hating myself, you see, has always come naturally; it was just my standard state of being. I woke up primed, each morning, with instant frustration that I hadn't miraculously improved during the night. My thoughts just as stupid, my flaws just as plain, my body just as disgusting as six hours before. I couldn't even slam a door on the cause of my anger. She was always there, on the other side, waiting to push my buttons evermore.

On some level, I recognised that this destructive mindset was all, well, in my own head. But that level was so far above where I generally operated that I needed a lift to access it. So the cruelty just continued, in a way that I would never have stood for had the victim been anyone other than myself. I didn't deserve to be treated with the same respect as the spider I rescued from the bath, because I was failing at life, while the spider was only struggling with it. If I had been pushed for a rundown of my best qualities, I wouldn't have managed beyond number one: succinct. Even on my healthiest days, when I managed to trample over anxiety and make it into society, I still did so with an ugly face and lack of personality holding me back.

And where exactly did those decades of mirror-shaming get me? Locked in a box with a head full of crackers and a spirit that all the king's horses couldn't heal. Looking back, I'm driven slightly crazy by my own carelessness; all that time, all that *life*, willingly surrendered to my very own jailor. Although, now, in a strange sort of way, the sentence was worth the release. I certainly wouldn't go back and do it all over again – there's only so much flagellation oneself can take. But in moments of quiet, when there's enough scope to contemplate the mire from which I dragged myself and the ground on which I now stand, that's when I really know freedom.

Those moments bolster me, they strengthen me, they urge me ever onwards.

Sometimes, I admit, I still really need them. I would love to say that I'm the picture of confidence now but, some days, I'm still not even the picture of a person who'll let a picture of her be taken. Those harmful opinions and beliefs are rooted so deep in my psyche that I'm not sure I'll ever dig them out completely. They've been with me through a lot, after all, and it's not easy to let go, despite how little they serve me. But my adventures have given me something that an immaculate complexion never could have – the ability to cope when everything isn't quite so rosy.

Dragging a scarred torso from infancy to adulthood would probably wound even the hardiest of souls. Or at the very least, give them a bad back. I won't go back over the details of my scalding injury, although, over the years, I've thought up a plethora of different phrases by which to describe it, some of which might be a bit graphic for print. Lumped in with all my other mental health baggage though, the physical damage didn't really give me a shot at a decent body image. My warped skin has been a constant reminder of what I'm not, and what I never will be. I'd never have a bikini body, since bikinis aren't made with burns victims in mind. Right from the start, I didn't have a chance to be perfect. As an adult, that goes without saying; as a teenager, it was said, again and again and again.

Even as my recovery from anxiety's thrashing became ever more stable, I still didn't imagine I would reach the point of being comfortable in my skin – particularly the misshapen parts. Was there really any way for me to find that sort of composure after an eternity of looking through quick-fix diets and hair removal treatments?

Actually, there was.

And all it took was a new dressing gown, a roomful of strangers, and two hours of sitting very, very still.

LIFE MODELLING

Air comes in jolting pockets, gulped into lungs filled only with the hope that this might be the last breath to come. I begin to twitch, to obsess, to fall into patterns so ingrained they have their own postcode. My muscles ache with the stress of prolonged clenching; readying to spring into flight the minute that fight loses out. The familiar pull of panic clutches at my chest, preparing to throttle again every ounce of my resolve. Not now. Please not now.

You can't do this, it screams; echoing so loudly around my frenzied head I'm sure the room will hear. Run. Hide. Die. You will never survive this. I grit my teeth and drop the robe.

Nothing happens. Well, nothing catastrophic. There's the noise of pencils rubbing delicately over paper, and the shuffle of a few resettling feet, but the solar system hasn't collapsed in on itself, and I'm managing to remain standing upright, if a little on the wobbly side.

Talking about the wobbly side, I'm very aware at this particular moment that, in forming a complete circle around me, some of the artists are being faced with mine. I've been advised by the class's tutor, Gareth, that models are expected to rotate after each pose in this first session, to give the students equal access to their subject's matter. For half an hour, the group will sketch quick outlines of dynamic poses, as a warm-up, although the variety of carefully angled radiators and my burning shame are keeping me pretty toasty.

Two minutes into my tennis-playing pose and I'm asked to change. Not because I resemble McEnroe after a hard five sets, but because I have another 11 positions to fit in before the break. I turn slightly, facing the next unfortunate onlooker, and ... and ... my mind goes totally blank. There are no longer any thoughts in there. It's like the aliens have finally landed and sucked all cognitive processes out through my ears. I have to come up with my next move soon because confused crouching is not an appropriate pose. A woman behind me sniffs; I hope it's a cold and not disgust.

Do something!

But I can't think up a single activity, and the nervous shakes have started, which, for a big busted bird puts some unwanted swing into the mix. From the doorway, Gareth waves, then pretends to be digging. I figure it's an instruction, rather than a cruel reference to the hole I'm in, and follow his lead.

Calm down, Paula. Only 10 more to think up. Be prepared next time.

And I am, with an inspired archery stance that leaves nothing to the imagination. At this point, I can imagine nothing worse than my current situation, showing off my every crook and nanny behind an imaginary bow and arrow; except perhaps for the poor sods sizing me up for the entire morning. There's a chap in the top corner with a canvas taller than I am so I dread to think what sizing is happening up there. By the break, I've successfully imitated a boxer, a seamstress and, what I think I meant to be a flamingo, and I'm finished with the most difficult part. My final hour of modelling is to be spent in one spot, seated on a stool that I hope is regularly sterilised, so the pressure of performing is at least reduced. But I still haven't calmed down.

I recognise when I'm in the throes of panic now, as soon as that blurring bubble closes in around me and I start to feel disconnected from my surroundings. In those moments, my brain is so inward-focused that it's no longer interested in external stimuli, and I slip through situations without leaving a trace. Maybe in this case I should gladly allow anxiety to rob me of the memory. There are probably others in this village hall who would quite happily give theirs back too, if allowed the choice. But I've worked too hard – and waxed too much – to let this one go.

I begin to pick out details around the room, noting them, counting them, connecting with them. A curtain fluttering in the air, a lopsided easel, the buzzing of the strip-light overhead. These tiny background features will cement me as part of the overall landscape; not separate, not detached, not alone. My breathing settles as I reach out to my environment for stability, still barefoot but reunited with my white dressing gown for the time being. I pad across the floor, taking the time and faking the courage to glance sidelong at a few of the drawings. The artists are keen to engage with me, pointing out where they've captured my likeness and where they've struggled. My hair recognisable in one, my cheeks in another.

The chat, the feel of the paper, the sight of my etched backside, all help to ground me in the space; refusing anxiety this experience for its own. This may not be my finest moment, but it will still be my own.

NEVER A CROSS WORD

Some people are there for the entire journey. Some are there just to kick you onto the right path. And that quick left foot can often be the most valuable input of the lot.

I once met a man called Calum. He was Digital Editor for a Scottish newspaper group and, for unknowable reasons, he believed in my adventures. He gave me an outlet – a blog for their site – and we became friends, as I pitched lists of ideas for my next everyday exploit and he smoked out of the window and told me I was mad. He thought the life modelling suggestion was both hilarious and poignant, given the juxtaposition with my past life, and less than a week later, I was stripping off for strangers. He had far too much class to offer to come along for the adventure.

We were an odd pairing. He, the lifelong journalist, with the knowing glances and gentle advice; me, wired and energetic – the puppy gnawing at his socks and sandals. Somehow, it worked as a friendship. Not in a sitcom kind of way; we didn't move in next door to each other and share ice cream after bad days at the office. But we did keep in touch and catch up when we could, and he began involving me in projects that meant something to him.

Eventually, the blog led to my first regular writing work: a weekly column on my adventures in a national paper. And while I'm pretty confident that Calum didn't bribe a guy to offer me the gig, I know that his investment in me said enough in those circles to have the same effect.

This isn't a eulogy – I don't have the skill or the right to attempt such a task. And no words could I put into a meaningful enough order to sum up a life so lived. All I can attempt to describe is the impact of his constant faith in me.

The last words I said to Calum, on leaving his flat after tea and more of his unfailing counsel were true and remain so, even after time has passed. 'I love you.' But what they weren't, was enough. I should have told him how much he had changed things for me. I should have explained that his opinions had meant so much. Instead, I just said what I always said, and hoped that he could intuit the rest.

That's the power of people though, coming into each other's lives and altering the direction of all next steps taken. I had unwittingly closed myself down to that input, and only now realise how much I missed out on: just another gift anxiety tried to steal away.

And it wasn't just Calum, although the impression he made could never be panel-beaten out. The kindness and giving of folk who have no real investment in how things turn out has overwhelmed me repeatedly, and changed how I approach every interaction with others. After all, you never know when you're being someone else's Calum.

Or when you're changing someone's opinion of themselves with some perfectly placed brushwork ...

BODY-PAINTING

My left boob itches.

Oh God, it itches. It tickles so much I'm beginning to shake. Uliana notices the movement and lowers the paintbrush. I look down at my royal blue flesh and wonder how on earth I'm going to scratch it. After four and a half hours of being decorated, there's no way I'm risking a smudge, so opt for just blowing frantically on the skin instead.

I smile apologetically, as Uliana gets back to work.

It's awkward. I mean, really awkward. You know when teenagers say that things are awkward and you know that they're exaggerating for dramatic effect? This isn't anything like that. At least at this point I have an outfit of sorts on – albeit one made entirely of paint and imagination. Somehow though, it makes me feel a little more protected. I'm basically the living embodiment of The Emperor's New Clothes.

The atmosphere is no fault of Uliana's. The artist has put everything in place to reassure her nervous canvas: a changing screen, hide windows, and flesh-coloured pants to spare my blushes – and her brushes. The set-up is as comfortable as sitting naked in a stranger's lounge could ever be. Well, as comfortable as sitting naked in a stranger's lounge being painted head to foot, with cameras pointed from every angle anyway.

Uliana's studio area is a cordoned off section of her home's dining room, which she uses to showcase her incredible abilities to turn human bodies into lions and tigers and, in my case, a pop art pin-up. Oh my. The cameras allow her to capture the process, as much as the end result, in all its time-lapse glory. Although I dread to think how having my belly sponged and speckled will look in slow-motion.

I lift my arm, as Uliana perfects the strap of my pretend top. The conversation has been flowing easily, even though, at times, the artist has a loaded brush pressed against my Netherlands, which makes thinking up topics somewhat tricky.

'So, do you like cashews?'

Her kids are playing upstairs, obviously quite accustomed to the situation, although once or twice now they've crept down to the hallway, and asked permission to come in to view their mother's latest exhibition. Each time, the answer has been clear, even though spoken in Russian – no bloody chance.

A final few brushstrokes to fix my smeared nose and we're done. Even though I've sat through every second of the five hours' work, it's hard to believe what Uliana has achieved with, let's face it, a second-rate surface on which to create. My body looks incredible: not because of my spectacular exercise habits or lack of modesty, but because somehow, with just talent and an array of art supplies, Uliana has buried all those pesky pounds and folds under a trick that even my eyes are enjoying.

I stand in front of a mirror, for the first time impressed by what I see. Spinning and peering, I'm forgetting to be bashful, even though, technically, I'm still not exactly dressed for the occasion – whatever the occasion may be. My arms and face are covered in pink dots, I have 'WOW' on my chest, and a green neckerchief knotted jauntily at my clavicle, and it's making me feel like an honest-to-goodness superhero. None of it is real, but my reaction is, and I won't be washing that away.

SHOW AND TELL

Exposure – of one sort or another – became a bit of a feature of my adventures over time. I suppose it started out as a test. I had reached a point with my anxiety that it took a lot to provoke it, and sometimes, weirdly, I wanted to find out just how much. So I poked the bear – or the bare, as it were.

The morning of my life modelling stint, I threw up so much they could have fashioned another model from the excretions. Being nude for two hours while artists size me up brings on anxiety. Good to know.

That first time I stood up to tell my story to an assembly hall of stony-faced teenagers, I could hardly hear myself speak over my inner voice's warnings that I wasn't going to survive. School visits trigger the nerves. Tick.

I'm aware that it sounds like a completely absurd way to spend my time, but making myself vulnerable, showing myself I can keep going no matter what, reminds me how far I've come and, I guess, how far I can still go.

I'll never forget the morning my father-in-law called me at work to ask if I'd seen that day's tabloid newspaper. I hadn't. Unfortunately, he had – and so had his workmates, as he'd opened up the paper on the lunch table, right to the place that my naked bum was printed across two pages. The article itself was sensitive and engaging; though typically, the picture desk had chosen the one photo from my blog in which I was showing any flesh other than my exhausted face. And there I was, posing in the buff on the art class stool, spread over the centrefold, for all to see.

I was mortified, but only for a moment. Then I recognised the embarrassment for what it was: just another facet of anxiety, trying to creep back into my world. I'd managed to rouse it from the depths again, and all it had taken was public humiliation and awkward Christmas conversations for years to come.

Anxiety will always be with me, in my adventures, throughout my life, but it doesn't have to be holding the reins – especially if I'm not wearing any.

SKINNY-DIPPING

It's a Tuesday in mid-November and I'm somewhere on the Ayrshire coast, in swimwear and sandals. The wind is cutting, coming from whatever direction it fancies, ripping through my enthusiasm for this escapade, gust by gust. My toes are already curling away from the water's edge, and I'm wrapping goose-bumped arms around my exposed midriff. They're my own arms, but are currently so numb they could be anyone's.

I'm afraid of the sea. I'm afraid of most water, but the sea has a name for being scary and I'm not about to take it in vain. Not that I'll be going further in than necessary to cover all my bits and bobs. My bits aren't bad, but no one needs to witness them bob on the water. This dip will be short and cold, much like the dipper herself. The beach here stretches as far on each side as my vision, but its sands are quiet today, thankfully. The odd jogger lumbers past, but who am I to call anyone odd, when I'm minutes from splashing my way into the waves, unencumbered by dignity.

Gerry counts me in, ready to capture the moment his wife leaves the safety of shore –and social acceptability. 'Three, two, one.'

There's a smile in his voice, but I'm too busy ripping off the Band-Aid of my bikini to turn and witness it. I know it's freezing but I'm too scared to notice, as I clamber into the water, one flip-flop already lost to the surf. I'm up to my waist and the icy ripples are reaching further with every step. So I stop, half in, half out of the swell, spread my arms, and just laugh, like a maniac. I've put myself in some ridiculous situations lately, and this one ranks highly – not quite human catapult, but not far off. The wind barrels into my chest and

I stumble, knocked down to one knee, the waves slapping my face. The spray does nothing to dampen my fun, but continues to dampen pretty much everything else I have.

Majestic sandstone houses line the promenade behind me, clearly built without this particular view in mind. I don't even care that their oriel windows face this way, or that, from such an angle, anyone on their balcony could see the seedy underbelly of this adventure as I'm tossed around on their doorstep. The water doesn't give a damn and neither do I.

Being out here is exhilarating. Terrified of being lost to the depths, but happy to draw the sea around my shoulders like a blanket. Chilled and bare and wild. I let myself go for just a second, stop fighting the tide and simply be. The steely fingers of the sea support me and I don't have to think or worry or decide.

The moment passes and I'm back, frightened and scrabbling for control. But I know that feeling of release now and I want it more than ever.

THINGS I LEARNT FROM BEING IN THE NUDE

- That blue looks good on me. It's lucky really, since it's the only shade my skin can turn in the Scottish climate.
- How little dog walkers care about a naked person running into the sea, when their pets are doing something cute enough on the beach to become an adorable profile photo. Aww, look at my bichon frise digging up that empty beer can. Click.
- That objects in the mirror may appear larger than they are. Or smaller, in some cases, I guess. Basically, perspective is a law unto itself – and Brunelleschi – so I can't trust to the horrors my eyes perceive staring back from the mirror.
- 2,860,854 multiplied by 83, and how easy it is to do mental arithmetic when trying to distract myself from the woman outlining my nipples with a fine paintbrush.

- The joy of pulling up beside a family car at traffic lights, while painted like a Lichtenstein come to life. Those three kids will always question the existence of mutual dreams – and their sanity.
- Not to always fight the tide. Sometimes it knows exactly where I should be.
- That my body is not something to be looked at or judged; it's an extraordinary piece of engineering that keeps my innards in and stops my head from rolling down the street.
- How delightful it is to be likened by an artist to a miniature Degas, and how quickly the delight dissipates when researching what Degas actually painted.*
- To be the worst I can be.

TO BE THE WORST I CAN BE

Like I said earlier, I didn't ever have a chance to be perfect. From almost the word go, I was damaged, and I wonder now if the universe was just trying to prepare me for the hell ahead. Really, I should have taken the hint and rolled with what I had, but it took me a whole lot of clutching at success to recognise the joy of failure.

Before someone reminds me that aiming high is important, I'll make it clear that I'm not down on aspirations. I'm a major promoter of shooting for the moon; think Don King meets NASA. I just believe we sometimes become a bit obsessed with the desired outcome rather than the process, and miss the wisdom that all the effort can bring.

Throughout my life until now, I made the mistake of only doing things that I knew I could do. It's a common pitfall, but I fell to it early

* Let's just say the lithe young figures I had expected his paintings to depict weren't quite what I found. I particularly like *After the Bath, Woman Drying Herself*; that dame has depth. It does make me wonder how exactly I was posing during that class though.

and just kept tumbling. I was academic and knew my way around an exam, so accepting a place at university was an obvious path, since I knew that as long as I studied, I had the ability to get by. But ask me to find a new hobby, or give a sport a go, and I would disappear from your line of sight quicker than you could suggest cross-country running. Anything outside the scope of my existing skill-set was just an opportunity for me to fail and to be judged by the people around. If I wanted to always be good at things, wasn't it just better not to try?

I'm not sure when we decided as a species that learning is only for the very young. When babies first start to crawl, we don't tell them they should just crawl forever because they look pretty good at it; we teach them to stand, to walk, to progress. At some point though, we stop encouraging each other to keep searching. In schools, teenagers are told that they're proficient in science or languages, so should just concentrate on that for the rest of their lives. We persuade them to stop looking, to stop expanding, to be content with what they're good at now. What happened to doing what you love? What happened to growth and development, to moving beyond what we are right now? Maybe we should ask ourselves what we want to be instead, then find out how best to make it there.

I grew up not realising that it was alright to be rubbish at things and to keep doing them anyway. Sure, I'd heard that it was the taking part that counts but I was better at the counting than the taking part, so decided to stick with that instead. Other people were talented at sport, and drama, and singing; I wasn't. So I left those things to the gifted, since I could never hope to be as good. I hadn't realised that the only person I should have compared myself with was my current self – and I could definitely be better than she was. I'll never be the best cyclist in the world, but I'm a million times better than Paula six years ago, just because I tried.

Nowadays, I try new things constantly, meaning that I fail at something or other pretty much every day. And it has been so good for me. I'm constantly putting myself in the situation that I'm the worst in the room, sky or ring, but instead of seeing these as opportunities to fail, I see them as opportunities to learn. If I'm in a boxing gym, every other boxer there is better than me, which means they all know something I don't, and I'll be damned if I'm not going to learn from every single one of them. I reckon it's time we all stopped trying to be the best at everything and embrace the times when we're the worst, because those are the times when we have most to learn. I'm not perfect. I never will be. But I've discovered that I'm actually pretty good at being imperfect – and I'm getting better every day.

CHAPTER 12

ADVENTURES IN THE OUTDOORS (GREAT, AND NOT SO)

There's so much rain, it's hard to find the air between droplets. We're basically just trudging through a falling lake right now, without sight of our mooring place. I'm still managing without my gloves, since they're in my backpack and I don't want to stop to fish them out, but another few hundred feet, and I know I'll need them badly. For the minute though, the effort to just keep trudging onwards is keeping the chill in my extremities at bay.

Ben Nevis, it seems, provides for its visitors.

I try not to look up. Not that I could see much, if I did. The typical Scottish weather is hanging around the summit, hiding our destination from all but assumption: it has to be up there, somewhere. Huck forges ahead, and I follow, weaving through a walking group that's taking over the entire path. Two hours in to our climb and I'm tired of everything bar the company. We've hardly spoken since our last pit-stop, just signalling that we're fine to carry on, but life tends to be stripped back to essential functions only, at this height. On the 120-mile drive back we'll swap anecdotes and laugh about me falling over, which I'm sure will happen before long, but, for now, I'm happy, as long as I can always keep sight of the badge on his bag up ahead. Even that is becoming more difficult, as the mist thickens around us – or cloud, I guess, as it's probably called up here.

'Okay?'

'Yeah. You?'

'Yep.'

One foot in front of the other, that's all I have to do; I don't have time to contemplate where I'm going, or worry about where I've been. And although each additional step is harder to muster, and my left shoe is letting in more water than is actually out here, it's strangely comforting to have nothing else to think about, but the mountain and my progress up its side. Since I first tagged along on one of Huck's Munro-bagging trips, I've found solace in the expanse of the hills and in the struggle to scale them. Whether clambering up or carefully picking our way back down, those moments of absolute focus, bookended by postcard views, are salve for any battered soul.

I stumble and grab hold of the rock face, scraping my bare palm. The route is well-trodden but uneven; in places loose underfoot, in others patchy and steep. And continually changing so that it's difficult to find any kind of rhythm. I use the interruption to rescue my gloves and wrestle my numb fingers into them. Huck hasn't stopped, and I smile to myself as I hustle to catch him up. This is what I love most about being out here; I'm completely capable, and I'm treated as such. Although we're a little team, scaling the mountain together, Huck doesn't expect any less of me than he does of himself. He's always looking out for me, as I am for him, but he won't be my crutch because he knows that I don't need one. He never met Old Paula, and the new one isn't a victim.

'Okay?'

'Yeah. You?'

'Yep.'

The terrain has changed again in these last few metres, and I hope we're finally nearing the top. My hair is sodden now; the wind blowing raindrops sideways, inside my waterproof's hood. This stretch of the trail is a relentless incline, just steady enough to allow a tiny increase in pace. Any walker we pass on their way back down reassures us that there isn't far to go. But since we've been hearing that same platitude for about the last 50 minutes, it's becoming hard for even this optimistic fool to believe.

'Okay?'

'Yeah. You?'

'Yep.'

Huck and I are side-by-side now, staying relatively close as visibility reduces to a stone's throw. And you haven't seen how badly I throw stones. I want to stop, I think, more than anything, but I'm still moving forwards so clearly there's something I want more.

In only a few hundred more paces, I finally reach it. The track flattens out and Huck points out the ruins of the observatory, as we try to shield our faces against the elements. Up here, the elements always win. Straight ahead is the cairn, and we take our turn to stand at its side, posing for photos against a backdrop of grey nothingness. I'm sure there's a panorama around somewhere, but we won't be seeing it today. I can't say that it matters though. Mainly because I can't really say anything while I'm breathing in freezing fog and drizzle, but also because just being on this 100-acre plateau, above the world, cut off from its complications, more than merits the three-hour hike.

There's a tiny emergency shelter on top of the old observatory tower and we edge our way inside. It could comfortably hold two budgies and the thin end of a wedge so obviously there are already five people inside. We make friends instantly, otherwise the seating arrangements would be considered assault, and Huck sets about his traditional cheese and jam sandwich reward. I've barely washed my flapjack down with the water dripping from my nose when it's time to go. The climate at this height can bear no relation to what's below so we've no idea what we're heading back to. Plus, we've promised ourselves a chip-shop dinner to top up the fat stores, and I don't imagine they deliver to this postcode.

'Okay?'

'Yeah. You?'

'Yep.'

And it's just one foot in front of the other once more.

ONE FOR SORROW

'Good morning, Mr Magpie.'

If you had shown me a picture of a magpie back in the day, I would have panicked, screamed my greeting, saluted, made my thumb and pinkie into a chain and broken it with the other pinkie, then asked what the hell you were doing in my flat with random photos of birds. You weirdo!

Since someone kindly told me the superstition surrounding magpies a few decades back, the two-tone crows have always sent me into a complete flap. At first, it was just the salutation, but gradually the protection routine grew arms, legs, and eventually a beak. I once almost crashed my car while going through the rigmarole, in order to avoid risking bad luck. Once I had started, there just didn't seem any reason not to do it. I mean, apart from the vehicle in front, who was I really hurting by continuing with the habit? And surely not having to worry about the consequences of angering the universe was worth the small cost of my time.

I can see now the pressure that anxiety was putting upon me to fall further into its debt, and that the cost of paying up was actually my failing mental health. That probably sounds melodramatic. Taken alone, my magpie custom was pretty harmless, but in conjunction with the touching wood, throwing salt, avoiding drains shenanigans, there was clearly something more underneath. Definitely don't sneeze around me, that's all I'm saying.

The superstitions were just another symptom of how much my inner workings were affecting my outer experience. And some of them remain. I still wouldn't choose to walk under a ladder, but now I'm more concerned about falling soap suds than any greater misfortune – my hair doesn't respond well to moisture. For the most part though, I'm no longer pandering to luck or any of its demands, and it isn't a huge victory to work out why. Learning to face life, in all its mountainous highs, and deep sea lows, has taught me to take control of my own reality and let go of the daft idea that I can control anything else.

Reconnecting with the world, being outside among its wildest places and people, reminded me how very small my one human brain actually is. For far too long, it had been my everything: insulating me, surrounding me, and convincing me to believe all that it said. I was in an abusive relationship with myself. Keeping me in line, through fear and doubt, were anxiety's chains, and to break them I had to start trying to see things in context, whether that was a black-and-white bird or a well-functioning drainage system.

Gradually, I realised that my thoughts, no matter how loud and obnoxious, couldn't always be trusted because there was so much they didn't know about the world, and more still they didn't know about me.

FREE HUGS

Buchanan Street, Glasgow.

Four days before Christmas.

Noon.

I've only just left the car park and already I'm shivering; the December wind cutting through to the very last of my layers. I'm only intending to be out for 10 minutes or so though, and even my cold blood can stand that.

There's a spot just down the road a little, that's right in the middle of the pedestrian section, surrounded by designer stores in what is known as the city centre's Style Mile. I think it's the perfect place to sell my wares – or give them away. The street is busy with the sights and sounds of the season, and I'm here to add the feels.

Standing small among the shoppers, I stop, raise my handwritten sign, and put on my hopeful face.

FREE HUGS.

I'm a pop-up shop with only hugs on the inventory and an immediate returns policy. My smile betrays my fear; it has always been disloyal. It's not easy to risk rejection in such a public arena, and I'm already starting to worry that, for someone with social anxiety, this might be the most terrifying challenge yet. I'd face a hundred hounds of hell rather than one set of eyes witnessing my humiliation, so why did I think this would be a good idea...

Before my sneaky brain can hammer home its negativity, a young man bounds towards me, all energy and cheer, to cut the ribbon unceremoniously on my adventure. Hugs are known to reduce blood pressure and this one is certainly having an effect on mine. Maybe the next nine and a half minutes won't be lonely after all. I thank him, and he tells me it's a great idea. Everyone could be doing with a hug at this time of year. It's good to hear, but the concept isn't mine, even if the scribbled signage is. People have been free-hugging across the world since the first campaign 15 years ago; I'm just spreading the love – and probably a few winter colds – around town.

No sooner have I let my first customer go than another is at the counter; actually, several others. A whole flock of huggers surround my pitch, laughing, and jostling, and opening their arms to me: a stranger. I'm not sure I've ever felt so welcome. The volunteers just keep coming: burly workmen envelop me completely, elderly gents squeeze softly, and even a few return customers take up the opportunity for a second embrace on their way back.

A few minutes go by without takers, but I'm so warmed by the enthusiasm – and body heat – so far to feel snubbed now. A crowd of teenagers are heading this way, one nudging another towards me. They offer a group hug in exchange for a photo with me and my sign. It seems a fair price; in fact, I definitely got the better deal.

Even those too busy – or shy – to stop mostly send waves and grins in my direction, or call out reasons as to why they won't be joining in.

'My wife would kill me.'

'I've already reached today's quota.'

'I'm on duty.'

Fair enough, Officer.

I know I've overshot my 10-minute schedule, but I was so buoyed by the reaction, I couldn't really bring myself to abandon ship so quickly. I've been here for over an hour now, waving to customers in the tearoom overhead, being fed sweets by kids whose parents are waiting in line, explaining to tourists that there really is no catch to the low, low price. After around 30 hugs, I gave up counting, since frostbite was threatening to break my best abacus, but I reckon I've given the best part of 150. And the real best part? I've also received them.

Just as I'm readying to take stock and head home, an older lady approaches me apprehensively and, as I hold her tightly for only an instant of my time, she whispers that she had been really needing a hug all day. You can put a price on most things, but the value of that free hug was beyond measure.

TRY OR TRY NOT, THERE IS NO DO

I apologise to any *Star Wars* fans out there for the mangling of this quote. I'm a great admirer of Yoda – he's a hero to people of my stature – but I think he got it wrong on this one. And, for long enough, I followed his lead.

The original line, in case you've managed to escape its omnipresence is 'do or do not, there is no try', and I see where he was heading with it, I really do. The Force, it seems, does not entertain doubt. For the rest of us though, who perhaps aren't really aiming to save the galaxy, I reckon the message is slightly reductive. Trying isn't a weakness, it isn't a hazard to be avoided; trying is a verb that can really take us places, if we get on board.

When choosing the name Paula Must Try Harder, I didn't give much thought to its meaning, or just how relevant to my situation it actually was. The phrase was a bit of a joke, a reminder of what my teachers had always thought of my sporting efforts, nothing more. Over time though, the words have become more than a silly pseudonym to me. It's what I'm most often called in schools. It's the remark used against me when I'm too tired to get out of bed.

It's also become the mantra that I truly believe saved my life.

Just to be clear though, I would not suggest telling your anxiety-suffering loved one to try harder. Please promise me you won't. In doing so, you will only earn yourself an argument, a meltdown, and the title of Worst Supporting Actor.

Anxiety, as I'm well aware I'm boring you by repeating, is a mental health condition that no amount of trying can cure. Trust me, if folk could just try their way out of the panic attacks and crushing uncertainty, they would be doing so with the might of a thousand terrors.

But trying, for me, was the catalyst for my recovery and, no matter what the little Jedi Master says, I don't think any of us should underestimate its power, never mind question its existence.

I had given up. Not only on trying, but on myself. The years and the anxiety had convinced me that all I had was all I could ever have: all I could ever be. And, while it's no Jedi's fault, at times we all suffer from ignoring the power of giving life a good go. By focusing only on what we can do, and not on what we can try to do, we instantly limit ourselves, *making our now our evermore*. At the time of writing, for example, I don't have a bestseller, and it's not something I can guarantee will ever happen, but I'm sure as heck going to try.

I'm already steeling myself for the backlash here, since I know I'm playing fast and loose with Yoda's real meaning, but sometimes slow and tight doesn't quite put a point across.

Sure, be determined to do, be sure that you will, but never forget to try.

STILT-WALKING

'You're a natural.'

I'm so surprised by the words, aimed in my direction, I nearly tumble from my stilts. I've never been a natural anything, other than disaster, so I stomp my way back around in an ungainly circle to check who else Ariel could be talking to. We're the only two people in the little courtyard and the gate was locked behind us, but I remain unconvinced.

My teacher is smiling a huge, encouraging smile, and nodding, as though she knows I'm doubting her words. Actually, I'm sure she probably does know, since I spent the first five minutes of the lesson explaining just how impractical a person I am – getting my disclaimer in early, in case there's an insurance issue up ahead. Ariel simply sat me down on the edge of her van's tailgate and talked me through exactly how well I was about to do, even though we'd never met before and I'd never tried on stilts for size.

That's the kind of person she seems to be though: instantly inspired and encouraging, ready to point out what will go right, instead of what might go wrong. It's quite contagious: like head lice but for enthusiasm.

I won't pretend I wasn't a bit nervous: I'm not much of an actor, even on paper. But it wasn't the thought of towering above the land that holds me close that made me anxious; it was the possibility that I might let down my cheerful coach. I'm more than used to being the novice in any given situation nowadays, and that only makes me recognise the effort it can take to teach this pig to fly.

Luckily though, this is not Ariel's first rodeo, and I am not her first clown. Before my legs gained the extra inches they have always desired, I was taken through ground training on how not to break myself in the event of an almighty collapse. Afterwards she just handed me the stilts. Two simple wooden pegs, with ledges for bold feet, and a roll of duct tape for attaching them to my shaking pins. Essentially, a basic first murderer's kit – motive not included.

'You're doing so well. Now wave!'

I wave to my imaginary audience, from high above their little pretend faces, and almost forget to keep moving. I'm reminded pretty quickly though when I almost topple, and resume my marching. This type of stilt doesn't allow for exhaustion: you stop, you fall. There's probably a metaphor for life in there somewhere, but I'm too busy concentrating to find it.

Barely five minutes after taking, very tentatively, to my extended feet, I'm walking almost comfortably, wearing the trousers of a chap from the top of a beanstalk. My movements are becoming more fluid, and I'm bowing and clapping with nary a wobble in sight.

I reckon it's less a case of nature and more Ariel's nurture that put me up here but, either way, I've grown.

THINGS I LEARNT FROM THE OUTDOORS

- That adventure isn't out there. If you don't take it with you, you'll never find it, no matter where in the world you go.
- The importance of being part of something bigger than myself, whether that's a community, an activity or the wider world. Anxiety cut me off from everything and held me so tightly in my own head that the fear was all I had. Figuring out that there was so much more than my crazy thoughts to rely on was a hard fought, but valuable lesson.
- That it's best to figure out the difference between left and right at the bottom of the mountain.
- How few of the really scary things in life are out there, waiting for me. And how many of them I'm taking out with me.
- That it's impossible to count the leaves on my favourite tree but the effect of trying is well worth the effort.
- How to get changed in a car park without flashing anything worth seeing.
- To recognise my limitations and, therefore, always carry plasters.
- That the only way to stop making mistakes is to stop living.
- To live life to the fool ...

LIVING LIFE TO THE FOOL

Don't laugh at me. Don't even laugh with me, in case I stop laughing first, and you're left laughing at me again. That's the attitude I always lugged around in the past and, trust me, it was exhausting. Chips weigh heavy on the shoulder.

At a family dinner, a new in-law remarked with a grin that this was the first time they had ever witnessed me eating. That was enough. I dropped my fork, pushed away my plate and declared myself full. The problem wasn't with the cuisine, of course. I love food, in spite of our troubled past. The problem was that someone had, accidentally or otherwise, pointed out my idiosyncrasy and put me exactly where I didn't want to be – in the frame for ridicule.

What a waste. Not just of food, which is surely sinful in itself, but of effort and worry and life. At home that evening, I chastised myself relentlessly for being so damn sensitive. I thought up what I should have said, how I should have reacted, and tortured myself again and again for the failing. And I was still hungry. The whole episode probably consumed a day and a half of my time: much longer than the entire meal would have taken, had I made it past the starter.

To anyone that hasn't been at the pointy end of a social anxiety episode, this probably all sounds a bit trivial – childish even. I can't help but agree. I've since watched toddlers behave in the exact same way, and probably for the same reason. I just didn't have the breadth of social skills to communicate my issue. Had I been able to say that I really struggled with eating in public, and was making a huge effort to just sit at the table, or explained beforehand that I wasn't keen on communal dining, so might just pick at my food, I'm convinced my family would have been understanding. But I didn't give them the chance because I didn't know how. So, once again, I left myself completely open to mockery, just by not being honest about my anxiety.

The best present I ever gave myself was deciding to become my own clown. Let's face it, I've always resembled one; clumsy and frizzy-haired with a blotchy complexion. I'd just never let myself enjoy the fact. I hid my ridiculous light under a big squirty bushel, trying so hard to not to be laughed at, that I forgot I could laugh too.

Now, I embrace my inner buffoon, and it's the happiest I've ever been. No more worrying what anyone thinks of my gaffes, as long as we're all enjoying the show. Mistakes and blunders are going to happen no matter what – particularly to me. The more people can garner a little joy from them, the more worthwhile my calamities become.

And, if nothing else, I'm constantly amused.

CHAPTER 13

ADVENTURES IN DANGER

I've never really feared much.

Stop it, I can hear you laughing from here.

I'm well aware that for the first half of this tale, I basically listed things that have terrified me over the years, and I promise this wasn't some elaborate hoax. Just let me explain ...

What I mean is, I've never really feared things killing me. I've been worried about judgement and ridicule, failure and flaws, and, yes, water and drowning, but it was more the flapping and flailing than the eventual death that caused me such alarm.

No, I've never feared much, but I've been anxious about pretty much everything. And there's a difference. They're related, sure. They feed into each other, time and again. But they're not the same, not really. We liken anxiety to fear because it's the closest emotion we have to describe what we're feeling. Even within these pages, I've conflated the two, using the words interchangeably to give some sense of what I was battling, but when you're afraid of something, you tend to know what you're running away from, even if it doesn't make too much sense.

I'll give you an over-the-top example to illustrate the point:

I'm worried about opening the door to the postman: anxiety.

I'm frightened to open the door to the postman because last week he spelled out "I NEED YOU" in stamps across the letterbox: fear.

Okay, I'm simplifying for effect, but I hope you're still catching the point I'm chucking around glibly. Fear, as an emotion and a response, can be completely healthy, and rational, and useful. It can remind us when to fight and when to fly the hell out of there, and it triggers our body's physiological functions that make those actions possible. Anxiety, at least in the way I experienced it, does exactly the same, but for no bloody reason whatsoever. So I'd find myself all geared up for escape, sitting on the sofa, without anything in particular to escape from, except the utter monotony of a life unlived.

Fortunately, I can mostly spot the difference now, and when anxiety tries to set off the fear response, I'm quick to check the corridors for a false alarm. Getting to know my enemy has allowed me to recognise how it does battle and, more importantly, the best way to defend against it. When I hear myself start to fret about carpets needing to be vacuumed, or how I'll ever cope with an upcoming meeting I see it for what it is: anxiety, using my busy mind as a way back in. And I close the door. Sometimes it takes longer to notice what's happening and I'll spend a day or so in the mire, trudging along, up to my armpits in stress. Then I remember all its tricks and how I've taught myself to see through them, and I give anxiety a little nod of respect.

'Good try, my friend, but not this time.'

Funnily enough though, through recovery I've learnt just how much I have to lose, and how much I don't want to lose it. I love not being dead these days! And that makes it hard not to care about hurtling myself towards it repeatedly. That's the great thing about mortality though; to appreciate it, you really have to test it.

PARAGLIDING

Ouch!

One of my thermal layers has become lodged in the wire of my bra and it's rubbing every time I move. Man, paragliding is perilous in ways that I just didn't expect. Another one, for this lightweight, is being too light in weight to keep my feet on the grass. Apparently, the wind has picked up more than expected so the lesson will have to be a little different for me than for the rest of the group – four men of average build.

The teenager in my head is over the moon. It's as though all those stupid diets and restrictions are suddenly being validated – I'm thinner than four average-sized men! The adult in my head is over the hillside, every time the instructor lets me go. I wish I'd eaten a few more carbs.

Already, the four other beginners are halfway through their ground training, laying out the wing and learning how to fall properly. This part of the course is imperative to teach us the basics of paragliding, while we don't have to contend with falling from a height. I'm having to be anchored to the ground though and, with the limited movement that's allowing, I don't feel confident about the next steps. But we're so exposed out here that if the instructor moves a hand from my harness, I'll be in the air before the air knows what to do with me.

'Okay, just untangle your lines like I showed you and spread out your wings.' My wing feels decidedly unprepared for being spread. I'm staring at a contraption of fabric, attached to a Gordian knot of string, and I've no idea which end I'm even meant to be dealing with. The others are chatting while loosening the cords in some kind of logical order that I think I must have missed. I try to copy their work but it's difficult to cheat when the teacher is attached to your side. For quickness, he helps me, while explaining why the apparatus is laid out in this exact manner. The others are waiting and I'm beginning to feel like the class dunce, even though no one's offered me a pointy hat to wear just yet. It's about all I'm not wearing; it's seriously chilly in this place where wind comes to blow, even in four layers and a borrowed flight-suit that's about three people too big for me.

One at a time, we're expected to take a jog down the slope, dragging our wings behind, to start learning the mechanics of steering and braking while still on almost-dry land. As I watch, the rest head off at a pace, bumbling down the hill in turn, with their gliding kit following behind, before the wing finds its way into the air. A bit of steering and it's back down to be gathered together and brought back up.

Perfect.

The instructor is hesitant to give me the freedom to try on my own, so keeps one hand on my side-strap. His concerns are justified when, on my first run out, my feet lose purchase almost instantly, I yank the brakes towards my knees and sail over the top of him to land, unceremoniously, on my incompetent ass. Luckily, I was taught to fall with style so when I'm hammering into the mud with all the grace of a bat in a blender, I can at least imagine what it should have looked like. My brain can hold onto calm, or instruction, but not both at the same time, it seems.

'Not to worry. Next time will be better.'

It isn't. I can't seem to stay upright with another person clinging to my clothing, and when I tumble I'm instantly caught up in the lines, making the rest of the attempt impossible. It's just not working so something needs to change and, we decide, it's time to lose my guy.

I'm nervous. I can't remember what's meant to happen after take-off. It will all come to me in the moment though, I'm sure. I can feel my legs trembling beneath the flight-suit and I'm not convinced I'm cold enough to merit the shivers, but at least I'm being distracted for the moment.

Club members continuously launch from further up the incline, and fellow novices one by one take their turn to fly the nest. Running, catching the breeze, wings inflating, a little lift and then ...

It's my turn.

The instructor nods; I'm clear to begin.

I start to stumble down the rise, feeling the lines catch behind me, and up it goes, all at once. In less than a heartbeat – and my heart is properly beating – I'm heading leftwards, off the hill, and towards a field of unimpressed sheep. But the wind is picking up and I can see power cables overhead; cables that are drifting closer and closer.

I'm not ready for this. If I pull the brake, do I just plummet? I can't think. I can't think. I'm sure I'm being yelled at to not climb any higher but if I knew how to stop that climbing, I wouldn't be in this mess. Just try something, before there's nothing left to try.

I tug on the brake. Is that the brake? I'm sure that's the brake.

Something is happening above me. I'm not looking up. I wouldn't know what I was looking at anyway. I keep tugging, more forcefully now. Something keeps happening. I allow myself one quick glance down, since it's the way I seem to be heading. I'm above the field, not far now but at a weird angle.

Down, down, down. I'm going to break a leg. I hope it's only my own.

I should be preparing to land. Bend your legs or whatever. But I've no time before ...

Ouch.

I'm on the grass. There's a sheep skull resting on its side to my right.

I think I know how it feels.

FIGHTING THE TIGER

Perhaps I shouldn't have put myself anywhere near those power lines. Reckless isn't the word, but since the English language hasn't come up with a better adjective for such blatant stupidity I'll stick with it for the minute.

I knew that I had no idea what I was doing, even before the wind caught my sail. I'd been given all the information I needed to make a safe attempt at flight, but not enough practice, and instead of flagging up that my brain doesn't convert instruction well, I just ran with what I had, and hoped I wouldn't be caught out.

Worse still, I considered trying again only moments later. A rotting sheep's head is not, it seems, enough of a hint for this girl. Thanks for the warning, universe, but I'm going to go my own way on this one.

Every step towards the start line was grudged. I wanted to walk away. It seemed logical to walk away. But I couldn't tell if I was walking away, or if I was running away. I'd spent so long making excuses to avoid things I didn't want to do and talking myself out of trying, that I had no way of knowing if my grounds for quitting were based in reality or in anxiety.

If I left without challenging myself to have another go, would I instantly feel the suck of regret, stealing away all of my new-found confidence? Would I beat myself up for the rest of the week, tormented by the fact that anxiety had won the battle after all my hard work?

I had no way of knowing.

The problem stemmed from my lack of context for danger. I'd grown up shielding myself so much from risk that I could see its shadow around every corner. My overworked brain couldn't figure out when I should be scared, since I'd never exposed myself to the experiences that would allow me to find out when I shouldn't.

Fighting a tiger, or going to a party: either seemed risky so I could just avoid both. There aren't many tigers in Glasgow. There are a lot of parties.

Through my adventures though, I had started to develop perspective on all those little things that I had been fearing for so long. But maybe I had gone too far in the other direction. Maybe I wouldn't recognise a real hazard if it bit me – or threatened me with electrocution.

My danger compass was wildly miscalibrated. Fortunately, there was another nearby of which I could make good use. Gerry had watched me dice with disaster and was more than happy to confirm that, while anxiety was probably chipping in too, this was definitely a situation I was entitled to walk, run, or shoulder roll away from without jeopardising my progress.

The paragliding episode was a pivotal moment for me in learning to trust my own instincts and to find the balance between adventure and safety. For a few months afterwards, I made sure to check my upcoming exploits with at least one person before leaping – or indeed galloping – into them ...

HORSE VAULTING

I'm standing on the back of a moving horse.

There's a horse, with a back, it's moving, and I'm standing on it.

No matter how I describe it, the situation doesn't seem to sound any less ridiculous. And yet, here am I, on this moving horse's back, standing.

Sure, I know that other folk – some as young as five – can somersault while swinging from a well-brushed mane; I've watched a few this afternoon. But for me – a person who can fall over while sitting down – this endeavour is surely just an arm waiting for its next big break. Helen, the club's founder and coach, has reassured me that I am, without doubt, capable of surviving my beginner's vaulting session unscathed. She's a friend so I trust her judgement, but she's seen how clumsy I am on two legs so I'm sure she can extrapolate to four.

Her confidence is unwavering though, and her coaching voice is stern, so I've just been doing what she says, and things seem to be going well so far.

And I'm still standing on the back of this moving horse.

Horses are tall. I don't actually know what's tall for a horse, but at 17.1 hands high, Oz isn't sneaking under any limbo bars. One of the long-term club members, Kellie, is up here with me, providing my shaky foundations with much-needed structural support, and I'm trying desperately to remember what we practised on the static barrel before my graduation to the real thing. But the real thing isn't fixed to the floor.

The real thing is cantering in a wide circle around the barn, tethered by its long lunge line, with Helen at the centre. Fine, it's sauntering in a circle. Okay, it's dragging its hoofs in utter boredom, but it feels really fast from up here. Our little unit meanders around the floor, while I try to gather my nerve for the next task: the dismount. Before carrying this load, Oz achieved some spectacular gymnastic feats; none more impressive to me than the perfect descent. Watching someone made presumably of the same stuff as I am, manoeuvre so elegantly with all the stability of a runaway train underfoot, to find her feet right where she expected them on the ground was joyful. Until I remembered that I was up next.

I'm still standing, and while I'm as proud of that fact as Elton John seemed to be, the only reason is that I don't know the way back down. Actually, I know one way back down, but I'd really rather not take it. Happily, Kellie has a good grasp on the sport – and my leggings – and she and Helen guide me down the tail end of Oz to land, more or less soundly, back on solid sand. My legs are shaky as I retreat back to the sidelines to watch another skilled performance from a boy half my age with double my confidence. Afterwards, he feeds Oz polo mints; a lovely part of the club's lesson plan to thank their steed for his fine service.

I psychically promise Oz all the mints I can afford if he can just make his back that tiny bit flatter, as I shuffle towards him for my final trick. Helen is keen for me to try something more technical. I'm keen to go home in a vehicle without blue flashing lights, but I know I'm not getting out of here without trying something slightly more exciting. Helen wants me to have the full experience of vaulting and, somewhere down below the fear and common sense, I do too.

By the time I'm standing on Oz once more, I'm sweating from places I'm not even sure have glands. A third passenger has joined us to steady Kellie, while I try to prepare myself for the manoeuvre. I've no clue how to prepare myself so just face the direction of travel and think really hard about polo mints.

Things are moving more quickly now. The pattern of the horse's steps has increased in tempo and my pulse with it.

'Ready? And jump.'

I'm not ready. I jump anyway, or maybe more hop. But whatever you want to call it, I've landed on Kellie's back without injuring horse or any of its riders. I somehow remember to breathe again. I look down. Everyone seems to be in the same number of pieces as we arrived in.

'Now stop holding on.'

I hadn't realised how hard I'm gripping Kellie's shoulders until Helen suggests I let go. It would be the ultimate flourish to end the routine: the gymnast's pose. I remove one hand, gingerly, taking it at least half an inch from Kellie's scapula.

I wobble. We all wobble. I put it back.

Once more around the barn, and I know this is my last attempt before Oz needs to rest.

Don't think about it.

I don't. I let go at once and throw both arms out to my sides. The breeze catches my hair and I can't suppress a grin. I feel like a circus ringmaster, playing to the crowd for the big finale. It's intoxicating.

But still I can't quite get over the absurdity of the scenario.

I'm being carried on someone's back on top of a moving horse.

This moving horse is carrying someone and their back is carrying me.

There's this back, right, and a horse ...

THE BEST OF THE REST

In case I haven't made this obvious, my adventures have shaped my recovery and the direction of my life these past few years, and it seemed a shame not to bore you with the details of a few more of my favourites, since you've already made it this far.

Guerrilla knitting: As bizarre as it sounds, guerrilla knitting takes all the leisurely craft of knitting and cranks it up to criminal. The theory is to turn urban landscapes into cosy art with handmade woollen wonders. In practice that's me and my mum knitting for three weeks, then creeping onto a football field early one morning to stitch 12 metres of plain-and-purl to the crossbar. Jumpers for goalposts, you see.

Random acts of kindness: Delivering chocolates to hospital staff and flowers to nursing homes is the kind of adventure that lifts the spirits, without having to leave the safety of solid ground. I also particularly enjoyed handing out bus fares to families and leaving coins in parking metres for harassed shoppers, with little notes wishing them a good day. It was one of the best for me.

Cage fighting: I'm not fond of being hemmed in, and I don't know how to make one of those fist-shaped things, so I can't say I was prepared for the onslaught of mixed martial arts in an octagonal cage.

Thankfully, I'm small and passive enough to go almost completely unnoticed, even in a two-person match. Being very, very good at looking completely pathetic also served me well in this setting. Cage fighters are surprisingly benevolent.

Ice climbing: On seeing the ice wall for the first time, I'll admit, not just my extremities went cold. 400 tonnes of snow, stacked vertically, just waiting for me to scale its side. But in climbing, as in life, add in a pair of toe spikes and some decent axes, and things get exciting. I can't imagine my technique looked particularly impressive from below, but no one fancied arguing the point with the woman with the weapons.

Slacklining: It's like tight-rope walking, except the rope is a line and it's not very tight. The whole business seems like a bit of a ruse, for wobblers like me to pretend we have a bit of balance. As soon as I put one foot on the line though, and felt it slide right back off, I realised my mistake.

Paranormal investigating: Midnight, in a cold, empty maritime museum on a stormy winter night. Armed with night vision cameras, spirit boxes and our wits, a team of investigators with this Scooby Doo as their tagalong, stalked the ships and hallways, waiting for spooks and scares. My wits left me after the first crackle of a spirit box. My bottle went soon after.*

Land-yachting: Think golf cart but with a sail and you're catching the drift, particularly if the drift you're catching is on a beachfront. When the wind catches, these wonderful little buggies can really shift so I had to hold on to the helm or I'd have been burying my shame in the sand before long.

* We didn't encounter any spirits that night, although there were some vague rumblings in the recordings. Maybe it was a crew member from one of the ships, drowned at sea. Maybe it was my imagination. The other half of the team had a wild night in the next building along, with furniture moving of its own accord and voices in the air. I told them how disappointed I was not to have been with them. I lied.

Beekeeping: 50,000 new friends, plenty of sweet stuff, and some natty headwear: what's not to love about apiculture? Fine, 50,000 stings might have spoilt my enjoyment slightly, but thankfully the swarm was subdued by a quick smoking of the hive before I met them.

Human slingshot: When I signed up to be strapped to an oversized catapult, winched back by a four-wheel-drive and launched into the air, perhaps I wasn't thinking straight. When I climbed back on for a second go, I wasn't even walking straight.

Bushcraft: Lighting fires in the woods did not sound to me like entirely responsible behaviour to begin with. I went along just to meet someone so bold as to advertise these services. Turns out, bushcraft is more about teaching people to light fires properly, with the safety of the trees, as well as the fire-starter, in mind. Eating berries from hedgerows in the west of Scotland really upped the recklessness levels though, since I've seen what they do in bushes around here, and it's not what you want in your salad.

Fencing: For most kids, being handed a sword and let loose on their peers would be Lord of the Flies. For the kids at the fencing club I joined, being handed a sword was just Wednesday night. And I was target practice. Apparently, I'm no more dangerous with a weapon than without, but, by God, can I rock a chest protector and face mask. Touché.

Fire-walking: Barefoot and wide-eyed, I padded across the burning embers of a once blazing bonfire with nothing on my mind except where to buy cushioned insoles. The trick is to focus all the excitement and nerves, and raise your energy to match that of the flames. Having feet like a troll's helps a lot too though.

FIRE PERFORMING

The paraffin catches. Flames puncture the winter dusk.

My hands grip the staff, feeling the heat thrust through the chill air.

Just as rehearsed, I roll the staff, flip it above my head, and watch as huge fireballs burn off the excess fuel.

An explosion of light and heat. I can't look away.

The staff is back in my grasp, so much heavier than before. So much more beautiful.

A modest crowd gathers, trickling from the nearby café. This small countryside retreat is oft entertained by life's elements. Tonight, I'll be the one harnessing them.

I've been practising for weeks for this moment. Practising fire performing without the fire. But now we've added the fire, and it's time for the performance.

I start with a rotor, then a figure eight, passing the staff behind my back, feeling the drag as the fire slows every motion with its pull and draw. The noise is nothing short of intoxicating: crackling, hissing, fizzing past my ears. The smell of burning fills my nose and, for a few minutes, my whole world is fire.

I can't see past it. Everything is ablaze. Maybe I'm on my own now. I don't care. I spin, and the fire comes too. I twist, and it's there, blazing circles around me, as I chase our centre of gravity, wherever it goes.

I'm not sure I'm still in control; the momentum guides my movement, the weight lures me around and around. Shadows rise and fall in our wake, and on we go.

The flames leave trails on my eyes, long after they've burnt their brightest.

THINGS I LEARNT FROM DANGER

- That the only power anxiety had over me was how easily it could convince me of that power. As soon as I began to question its authority, and see it for what it was, its hold over me loosened – and it has never taken control again since.
- The difference between being on fire in the movies and actually being on fire. Note: they look nothing alike.
- That I can trust myself to cope, and to carry on coping for as long as it takes.
- To always listen to instructions, especially when I have a parachute strapped to my back.
- How little I know about horses. For one thing, they don't even seem to recognise the Black Beauty theme tune.
- To remember that even when I'm at my best, the world will land a few blows, but as long as I learn from the damage, the bruises are always worthwhile.
- That it's always best to face fears head on. Unless the fear is of porcupines.
- To rest, even when I don't think I have time, because that one moment of calm is what will power me through the next 10 of turmoil.
- How quickly anxiety abandons me when I'm tackling real risk. Off it scurries to cower in the back of a cupboard in my brain, until the coast is clear for it to be the main event once more. Some day soon, I intend to lock it in there.
- That I am not fear.

I AM NOT FEAR

I am anxious. I am afraid. I am worried.

The words fall from my mouth as easily as a broken filling. I've said them so many times, my tongue has muscle memory. They probably weren't the first words I ever uttered, but they're up there with the most used ever since.

Even now, after everything I've gone through to battle back from life's very edge, I still catch myself, more often than I'm planning to admit, speaking these lies about what and who I am.

I am anxious. I am afraid. I am worried.

They're not true. I am none of these things. I may be feeling them – sometimes all at the same time – but they're not who I am. They no longer make my decisions or curb my progress. They don't even factor, most of the time. And they sure as hell do not make up the biggest part of me, so how can they possibly sum me up in any way other than poorly?

I am feeling anxious. I am feeling afraid. I am feeling worried.

I guess it might seem pedantic to make this distinction. Words aren't always spoken with the same care they deserve, even to ourselves. But I've noticed the difference they can make to my outlook, one way or another. Telling myself that I am anxious, makes it feel like a part of me, something immoveable and innate, that I can do nothing about. When instead I remember that I'm only feeling anxious, I can separate the emotion out, and know that it will pass. Feelings are fleeting, changeable, and don't ever need to be part of my permanent record. I can feel them while they are around, then move on because they are not an immutable part of me and never will be.

I'm certain that if you now decide to go back, and re-read anything I've written, you could count several instances of me falling back into these old language habits – and, I promise, I won't remove even one in the edit. I hope that you'll excuse these slips and see them for what they are: the honest mistakes of someone who pretends to be nothing more than a woman still breaking free from a lifetime of negative patterns and behaviours.

I am not anxious. I am not afraid. I am not worried.

I am not fear.

I am Paula.

CHAPTER 14

ADVENTURES IN THE FUTURE

The water trickles into my wetsuit. I feel its sharp coolness at my neck. A duck stirs in the nearby reeds. I wonder if it recognises me for what I am: an interloper in its domain.

As fish go, I'm a very small, and still quite scared, one in a very big pond. A loch, more accurately, somewhere in Stirlingshire. I'm the only one here as far as I can see, except the wildfowl and the lesser spotted husband, taking photographs of the distant hills from the safety of land. Even the usual sprinkling of fishermen have abandoned ship for the season.

The day is calm, with blue sky reflecting in the loch's stillness. But this isn't a summer scene. The cloudless morning has brought a frost in the air that bites at my face, below my natty pink swim-cap. The weather doesn't bother me. In fact, its changeability, and that of the landscape, is what keeps me coming back.

I paddle a little further and stop, watching the ripples creep ever outwards from my spot. I try to count the widening circles, but drift after the sixth. Just the act of counting though, or of watching, or listening, connects me to this place and pulls me from inside my head. That's the difference out here, and why it's become so good for me. This is my happy place: a place that I stole from anxiety and that I'm never giving back.

Something brushes past my leg as I float around, acclimatising to the temperature. It's only a few degrees above freezing and my extremities are starting to lose feeling. But that's alright. I'm feeling enough for all of us right now.

The journey here has been such a long one. Not in distance: I'm barely an hour from home. In recovery terms though, it has been light years, and dark years, and years of furious effort. Half a decade of lessons – almost a third of them just to prise me from the safety of the changing room – phobia counselling and a few verrucas later, and I'm somehow in open water, on my own, through choice. Isn't human capacity for change truly astounding? And there's so much more ahead.

Not so long ago, even just standing on the stony beach by the water's edge would have been too close, and already I would have begun to feel my legs weaken and my breathing quicken. Tears would have pricked my eyes. And then panic, in all its might, would have descended, stealing me from the beauty of this scene. Not only would my day out have been ruined, but the rest of the week, as I came to terms with the episode and moved to the next phase of self-destruction: attacking myself for the failing and my inability to cope. The change didn't come easily but now, just swimming in this stunning expanse, I know for sure it was worth the work.

I've only been able to call myself a swimmer for a few months, without having to lie. Even before I'd managed to put the breathing into my weak front crawl, my coach recognised how much difference being outdoors would make to me. Truly terrified, but trusting to his experience, I cried and flapped my way into the 30-feet deep quarry, holding on to him so tightly it was borderline inappropriate. I had never even been in the deep end of a pool before. But something gave way in my fear that afternoon. Things shifted around in my brain to make room for the possibility that maybe, just maybe, I could do this. And, boy, did I need that room.

You see, when I was taking that huge leap out of my phobia and into the open water, I had already decided to take on my biggest challenge yet … overcoming a lifelong fear, learning to swim, and plunging into a quarry was just the start of my training.

My next adventure will test me beyond anxiety, beyond myself.

For now though, I ground myself in the loch, in the ripples, in the chill, and just keep going.

THE BIG, MAD SWIM AROUND BRITAIN

One scared swimmer + six months + 1,800 miles of coastline = The Big, Mad Swim Around Britain.

From April 2018, follow Paula "Must Try Harder" McGuire, as the recluse turned adventurer takes on her toughest challenge yet – attempting to become the first person ever to swim all the way around mainland Britain.

A recovering aquaphobic, who spent 30 years unable to break a sweat without worrying about drowning, Paula will test herself beyond the limits of reason – and safety – to show that, while anxiety makes life hard, adventure makes living possible.

From Land's End to John O'Groats and all the way back around, this novice swimmer will tackle Britain's unforgiving coastline, powered by a passion for mental health awareness, cake, and hopefully a few friendly seals along the way.

Support her. Join her. But, whatever you do, please don't splash her!*

* She really doesn't like that.

EPILOGUE

I sip my tea and make yummy noises. The older man at the next table smiles.

'Enjoying that?'

I really am, and I admit as much.

The café is busy with shoppers and workers from the retail park. I'm sitting by the big window, in full view of passers-by, not because there were no seats at the back, but because this is where I want to be. There's no reason for my visit. I'm not meeting anyone. The coffee shop isn't on my way home. I'm not even sure I wanted a drink. I just fancied a win today, and this is always a lovely way to remind myself that I'm doing just fine.

This isn't my first time in a café on my own. No, that was last year. I was 36 years old. I was married and self-employed. I'd flown a plane and presented a radio show. I'd battled fears and demons and Olympians. I'd competed in a triathlon without being able to swim. I was a goddamn adventurer.

But I had never had tea on my own in public.

It sounds like such a stupid, trivial, nothing of an experience. People do it every day, in lunch breaks and snatched moments, all over the country, all over the world. But not this girl. Not ever. I had convinced myself that there wasn't really any need to do it. After all, there's never a shortage of tea at home, and I'd already shown that I could face even my biggest social fears, so what did I really need to prove? The answer, of course, was that I didn't have a thing to prove, but I still had a thing to face and that was impetus enough.

Every so often now, I repeat that first trip. Sometimes in the same venue, sometimes elsewhere. I don't take my book from my bag, or my phone from my pocket; I've cut my waist-length hair so I can no longer hide behind it. I look around, I drink the full pot of decaf, I hum tunes along with the clanking coffee machines. And I remind myself that this is how far I've come.

It's been an incredible few years of excitement and adventure, and those big, jumping, flying, bouncing moments will forever bolster me when difficult times come back around. But this, right here, at this wobbly little table with the sticky marks at the corner, is how far I've really come.

I'm not sure if I've mentioned this but I have social anxiety. Yes, even now. The people stuff in life is still difficult for me, but now I see its challenge and I raise it one of my own. Try to take me down, anxiety. I dare you.

Sometimes it does, and I let it have its day or its few days. All the while, I surround myself with those thoughts and tokens of my progress – the medals and photos and pinched memorabilia – and I climb back up, on top of my successes, and push forwards. I haven't cured myself of anxiety. What I have done though is give myself the upper hand in our constant battle because I no longer feel the need to fight.

I can handle it, whatever it brings into the ring, because I've prepared myself. I don't need to make the world an easier place to be. Instead I've made myself stronger, by throwing myself into its clutches and coming out bruised but alive, time and again.

I've bought a muffin; more as a symbol than as something to eat. Although the eating is a nice by-product. I bite into it, messily, without picking it into smaller chunks first; the crumbs gather around my mouth, but I leave them there. It's all part of the game.

Am I embarrassed yet? Am I feeling judged? Will I even notice if I am?

A woman opposite looks at me sidelong. I wipe away the crumbs. I'm in recovery, not nursery.

It's going well, mostly. Two years ago I stopped self-medicating, and all the chemists within a 25-mile radius went into liquidation. I still blink more than is probably necessary but at least I'll never have dry eyes. And I talk more than anyone I know these days; I reckon I'm making up for the 20 years of not speaking to anyone. I have a lot of excess words to use up. The big swim is only a few months off now and, sure, enough, the stresses are building nicely, but if they weren't, I'd be having my nervous system checked for malfunction.

Life is good – not perfect – but I've learnt to stop dragging around that impossible yardstick. Life will always measure up short. Nothing is as I expected it to be, or as I ever could have hoped. But I'm in a place I never thought I would reach, living a life I never imagined I could have, and if I didn't think that was worth trying hard for, I probably wouldn't deserve it.

I drain the tea and stand, buoyed by another ordinary moment of victory.

Adventure comes in many forms and I'm ready for my next one.

ACKNOWLEDGEMENTS

Adventures such as these don't happen on their own. There are so many people who have supported, strengthened and inspired me, and I'm pretty sure I wouldn't have had a story to write without them. They know who they are, but now you can too.

The McGuires, for never making me feel like anything other than part of the family.

Patrick and Isaac, my wonderful nephews, for giving me cuddles, even when you didn't want to. And for not being taller than me quite yet.

Tess, for never minding that we had to sit in the corner.

Seamus, for telling me I was made for bigger things, even though I never believed you. I hope this is big enough.

The Gesh family, for making me laugh, always, and for keeping me company in my darkest times.

Jeff, for the walks, talks and soup shared.

Paul Wright, Thomas Hamilton, Stephen Morrison and all those who convinced me that I was capable, in spite of the evidence otherwise.

Chris, my editor, for putting up with the many quirks of my writing – and for the privilege of calling you my editor.

I could never thank any of you enough, but I hope this is a decent start.

the Shaw mind
FOUNDATION
Creating hope for children,
adults and families

Adam Shaw is a worldwide mental health advocate and philanthropist. Now in recovery from mental health issues, he is committed to helping others suffering from debilitating mental health issues through the global charity he co-founded, The Shaw Mind Foundation. www.shawmindfoundation.org

Lauren Callaghan (CPsychol, PGDipClinPsych, PgCert, MA (hons), LLB (hons), BA), born and educated in New Zealand, is an innovative industry-leading psychologist based in London, United Kingdom. Lauren has worked with children and young people, and their families, in a number of clinical settings providing evidence based treatments for a range of illnesses, including anxiety and obsessional problems. She was a psychologist at the specialist national treatment centres for severe obsessional problems in the UK and is renowned as an expert in the field of mental health, recognised for diagnosing and successfully treating OCD and anxiety related illnesses in particular. In addition to appearing as a treating clinician in the critically acclaimed and BAFTA award-winning documentary *Bedlam*, Lauren is a frequent guest speaker on mental health conditions in the media and at academic conferences. Lauren also acts as a guest lecturer and honorary researcher at the Institute of Psychiatry Kings College, UCL.

Please visit the link below:

www.trigger-press.com

Join us and follow us...

@trigger_press

@Shaw_Mind

Search **The Shaw Mind Foundation** on Facebook

Search **Trigger Press** on Facebook